Thank You for reading this Book.

You are a true Blessing!

love Jo

Go For It!

A Woman's Guide to Perseverance

Jo Hausman

Published by Best Seller Publishing®, Pasadena, CA
Best Seller Publishing® is a registered trademark
Printed in the United States of America.

ISBN-13:978-1530139804
ISBN-10:1530139805

This publication is designed to provide accurate and authoritative information with regard to the subject matter covered. It is sold with the understanding that the publisher is not engaged in rendering legal, accounting, or other professional advice. If legal advice or other expert assistance is required, the services of a competent professional should be sought. The opinions expressed by the authors in this book are not endorsed by Best Seller Publishing® and are the sole responsibility of the author rendering the opinion.

Most Best Seller Publishing® titles are available at special quantity discounts for bulk purchases for sales promotions, premiums, fundraising, and educational use. Special versions or book excerpts can also be created to fit specific needs.

For more information, please write:
Best Seller Publishing®
1346 Walnut Street, #205
Pasadena, CA 91106
or call 1(626) 765 9750
Toll Free: 1(844) 850-3500

Visit us online at: www.BestSellerPublishing.org

DEDICATION

I dedicate this book to my God, my wonderful mom and son Cody, my dad, my late husband Jim & all of my wonderful friends and family who never gave up on me. Love you all.

Table of Contents

Foreword by Cody

Tragedy has a way of making us stronger, wiser, and more empathetic. Yet, often, these misfortunes are treated as taboo subjects; we don't talk about them much, which doesn't allow us to help people and be a source of strength for them. Our family's tragedy was shaped greatly by my mom's strength and courage throughout our ordeal. Like so many things in life, it was the timing of the situation that added the greatest meaning. So much was happening in our family at that time: graduation, moving, and new beginnings. It seemed hard to believe we were also holding onto hope that my stepdad, Jim, would live long enough to receive a liver transplant. All of the responsibility for these events fell squarely on my mom's shoulders.

Instead of letting emotion and grief get the best of her, Mom rose to the occasion with poise and dignity and led us through this sad and difficult time. It's one thing to know that your husband might die soon, but having your husband's fate hang in the balance is another thing completely. This is a nerve-racking experience, one that is shaped by health, politics and the decisions of doctors. It's completely out of your control, and you need to have faith in a higher being to reassure you.

She was always resolute in her belief that everything happens for a reason. She was determined to not give in to pessimistic thoughts, and that's what allowed us to come out of our grief stronger, and more understanding of what it means to live a full life. My mom's response to this loss was shaped by the fact that she lost her dad at a young age, and had overcome this tremendous type of loss before.

She lost her father at age eleven and her husband at forty-two, both atypically young ages. She was wise beyond her years, anchored by her faith in a higher power, remaining positive, and never giving up. But most importantly, she never let a moment of her life go to waste. With the loss of her husband (my stepdad), my mom could grow into an even more tremendous and caring person. She was empowered to put her energy and focus into her business ventures, to succeed and provide for her family -- especially now that she would be the sole provider of income. These experiences shaped her character and allowed her to be a source of strength for others dealing with similar losses. This is the beautiful upside of tragedy; that after the storm passes, there is a tremendous light that shines through.

During a funeral, you'd normally expect the widow to grieve the most and receive the most sympathy. But at Jim's funeral, Mom set her own interests aside and consoled Jim's family members. She had to be that caring person for them.

Mom was resilient. She could keep up with her business ventures; this return to normal life helped her get through. It's hard to go through a tragedy and rebound if you don't have the resources. Mom's business savvy helped keep our family afloat. Her example inspired me to be entrepreneurial, not in just a limited business sense, but in a "life sense:" to take care of what needs to be done, whether it be business, family matters, or social matters. She told me I should create something that can be my own, including being my own boss and controlling my schedule.

Her business was structured in such a way that she could take time off as needed, and not have to worry about the office. I wanted to follow her example in this area.

That's one of the biggest reasons why people lose it, because they don't have a feeling of control. That's something she maintained throughout the whole thing, which helped a lot. She always did have a sense of control, because she had these businesses that she was running, which created a cash flow so we had the resources to do things like miss some work. I had to have surgery, which required traveling back and forth to Omaha, Nebraska eight or nine times during the summer. It was a hectic time; it was a five-hour surgery during which I had both my jaws broken to fix an under-bite. The surgery was scheduled for the summer after I graduated from high school.

It all happened at once. Jim died right after I had major jaw surgery and my jaw was bandaged shut for eight weeks. At his funeral, my face was still incredibly swollen. It was crazy. During the summer when Jim died and all the drama took place, Mom and I must have gone back and forth to Omaha eight times, driving at least three hours each way. It was intense.

Introduction: My Why

I'm writing this book to help women entrepreneurs overcome obstacles in their lives, such as death, divorce, suddenly having an empty nest, or any kind of traumatic life changes they've experienced. Communication is key in work and relationships, and the lack of it can change a situation drastically. When relationships end, we can be pulled down into a very vulnerable situation. People will come into our lives for a reason, but they also leave for a reason, and sometimes we never know why. I have learned to trust God, knowing everything will work out with his timing and His plan.

Change is hard; but how we deal with each of these changes is how we propel our lives forward. I have overcome many obstacles in my life, the biggest of which came in July 2010. My life as I knew it was over. I had to pick up the pieces, brush myself off, and move on. The attitude I chose to keep while everything was happening is what has propelled me to where I am today. I've experienced tremendous growth since then; but it hasn't been easy.

Women entrepreneurs have to be strong-willed to overcome obstacles. We need strength, determination, perseverance, and fortitude. This book will help you with that. With all the challenges of life happening around us, we still need to keep up with work. Many women reading this book have a desire to work from home. Maybe some are already doing some work from home. Others are working a full-time occupation and trying to manage a home-based job. Starting a home business takes guts and determination, and when life is happening it seems pretty far-fetched to undertake it or keep it going. However, as the saying goes, where there is a will there is a way. It is doable and very rewarding once you take that leap of faith.

I started an at-home, virtual assistant business in September 2005 and never realized what a blessing it would be. To say I was scared is an understatement. I was petrified, but my fears lessened as I networked for myself and my business and told people what I was doing. I used the phrase "fake it till you make it" a lot back then. Many times I didn't know how to do certain tasks my clients requested so I researched and taught myself. I was determined to succeed.

The main reason for me to work at home was that my son was still in middle school and needed his mom at home. I wasn't able to stay home with him when he was younger, so this was the biggest blessing for me. Then, in July of 2006, my mother retired and moved to the same town we live in. She still lived independently, but her vision had deteriorated so she gave up driving. Then to top it all off, in November 2007, my husband learned that he had a deadly disease. Can you say "stress?" I know I can.

When my husband was in the depths of his sickness he spent much time in the hospital. My son was in high school at the time and I really wanted him to have a normal childhood. There were days I would sugarcoat my husband's condition so my son wouldn't know. Was this the right answer? Probably not, but at the time it made sense to me. I figured if I sugarcoated it, things would go back to being okay and we could be a whole family again. It didn't work and it was wrong. To be honest I didn't realize, or I didn't want to realize (or better yet, *admit*) how sick he really was.

People say I'm strong and can do anything. Some days *strong* is all there is, or rather I appear strong on the outside while being ripped apart on the inside. But knowing that drives me. On days when strong is a mere word, action has to be put into place to drive me to greater destinations. Some people call it being stubborn; but I call it determination. It's kind of like defiance against the expectation that you're going to break.

We are all fighting a battle of some kind. Early on in my adult life I decided that being positive was the way I wanted to feel and express myself. From my viewpoint, people who remain positive have a greater chance of surviving and thriving than those with a less-than-positive attitude. Perseverance and positivity are key attributes to have in order to endure this thing we call life.

Overcoming obstacles is part of being human. We all have to do it. How we handle it and perceive it is what makes us who we are destined to be. I have had countless hours of worry over finances, health, happiness, and family. All it did was give me gray hair and lose sleep. So once I decided to attack life with a positive attitude and to keep smiling through good times and bad, it made life worth living. Everything is temporary, including our lives here on earth.

My six-word mantra is *always hope, always peace, always love*. This story is about my life and how I overcame the obstacles that have put me where I am today. I'm not perfect and neither is my life. Although we all have obstacles to overcome, define your dreams, put your actions into steps, and get ready to go for it. My wish for you is happiness, hope, peace and love. I hope you find in this book the encouragement to keep fighting, keep living and keep loving. Life is grand no matter what obstacles you're facing…and it's time to take it back!

CHAPTER 1
Communication and Vulnerability

DISCUSSING MY deep personal feelings doesn't come easily for me. Showing vulnerability is tough. I think communication became tough for me the night of December 9, 1978. That is the night that my tall, dark-haired, handsome and fun-loving dad passed away from a massive heart attack. How could the man I adored who was full of life, vitality, vigor, and laughter lie there in a coffin and not move? The man I shared a birthday with would no longer be laughing or sharing my birthday with me. I was eleven years old at the time and was in sixth grade. He was the coach of my softball and basketball teams. He was my prince and I was his little girl.

My dad always had a smile on his face and laughter in his voice. He loved to make people laugh. He wrote poems and drank beer. We lived close to the Governor's mansion when we lived in Pierre, South Dakota; he worked for the state and he would walk home for lunch some days. I was allowed to go meet him if the weather was good. So when I was given the okay, I would walk toward the mansion and meet him halfway. He would greet me with a big smile on his face and ask me how my day was going. I treasured those times.

In addition to my dad and mom, I have two older brothers. I thought we had the perfect family. I rarely saw my parents fight. They loved each other more than life and raised us kids with great Christian faith and fellowship.

When he left us, my world as I knew it was over. I was shattered, scared and felt unsure of the future. There were so many people at our house crying and sharing stories of him. I remember thinking I just wanted all of this crying to stop and laughter to begin again. Our family used to laugh a lot and Dad liked to make jokes and make us smile. Two nights after he passed, I sat in the living room with my legs curled up under me, thinking if it was just five years from now, life would be good and we could laugh again. I longed to have a happy family again. I wanted to get back to a "normal" life, whatever that might be.

Crying shows vulnerability. It can strengthen us, hinder us or propel us. Crying is essential to healing. Laughing is essential to healing. The grief process affects each of us differently and we handle it in our own way. At the ripe age of eleven, I didn't know what grief was. All I knew was that I didn't want to cry anymore. Crying meant sadness and I wanted happiness. I wanted to be the strong one and console others instead of letting others see me cry.

My friends were kind to me and would give me a hug if I was having a bad day. My family was extra careful to be nice to each other as each day was a new day without him. My dad was the youngest of his siblings so it felt so unreal to everyone that he had passed away at the age of forty-four, leaving behind a wife and three children.

Nothing changed, except everything changed. Our lives were no more with my father and mother as parents; but now with Mom being in charge. She was a rock star and rebounded as quickly as she could to keep our lives as normal as possible. My mom is a wonderful example of what a mom should be. She didn't know how to be a single parent; but she gave it all she had.

Thankfully, we didn't have to move. We stayed in the same school and support system. She made the decision to raise us alone without the help of another man and for this I give her much credit. Raising three teenagers by herself was not an easy task. My teen years were awesome and that is because of the wonderful mom she was.

Two weeks after my father passed, it was Christmas. My mother was very efficient, so the tree was up and she already had presents with his name on them under it before he passed. It was hard to see those. Mom removed them from under the tree and decided to give them away. I also remember when it was time to give away his clothing. The smell of my dad was still on some of them and I never wanted to forget that smell. One of his favorite overcoats went to a cousin of mine who was in his twenties. I'm glad it did as he reminded me the most of my dad in appearance.

The rest of my sixth-grade year was kind of a blur, but thankfully it came and went and I was ready to go into middle school. I didn't talk about my dad to a lot of people. I didn't want to cry in front of others so I avoided the topic. When I did talk about him, it was always at happy times when I could laugh.

The first year without him was tough, especially on our shared birthday. My grandma (his mom) was still alive so we celebrated with her. Then I had a party with my friends. Even though friends and family were near, I still felt alone without him there. After that birthday party, I made the conscious decision that I would celebrate our birthdays for the both of us and would be happy about it. I have done that to today, and now celebrate our birthdays all month long.

The first summer after he passed, we had a different coach for softball. I hated him because he wasn't my dad. This man yelled at me for a play that I missed. I couldn't help but think if my dad was here he would have never yelled at me for that play. I cried to myself and couldn't wait for softball to be over that year. Living the first year after a loved one passes is a big adjustment and not an easy one. The year of firsts is hard: first Christmas without them, first birthday, first New Year, etc. With each stepping stone, we learn to adjust to living without them.

As the years went on, I continued in softball and other sports. In eighth grade we got a new softball coach; who was my friend Wendy's dad. He coached us through our high school years. He was my angel in disguise. He rarely got mad and always encouraged us, just like my dad would have.

Propelling through the school years after my dad's passing was tough at first; but it got easier. The more time that passed, the easier it became. They say time heals all wounds and I believe they are right. We don't forget; but the pain lessens.

When I was in the eleventh grade, my mother was asked to write an article for a local magazine about becoming a single mom after the death of a spouse. It described the events leading up to his passing and how my two older brothers and I reacted to it. She described how each of us reacted to his death, and when I read a part about one who got really quiet, I asked her, "Who was the quiet one?" I was surprised to find out it was me! I had little recollection of being quiet; it must have been a subconscious reaction to the grief. She told me how worried about me she was at the time and was trying whatever she could to get me to open up. I don't have any recollection of this except wanting to hide when someone would bring up the subject.

One thing I do remember was standing in line in grade school a few months after he passed away. We were eleven-year-old kids fidgeting in the cold and wanting to go inside. Someone in line said, "Why aren't you talking?"

Another girl said, "She just wants attention because her daaad died." I remember being so embarrassed I wanted to run and hide. The attention I got was humiliating to me.

After we got inside and sat at our desks my teacher asked me if I was okay. Oh my gosh. What was he thinking when he asked that? I sank down into my desk and almost cried.

Grief hits each of us differently and children react to it a lot differently than adults. My friends didn't understand because they all still had their dads. They were kind and gentle-hearted toward me, but still they didn't understand.

There were times when I would get jealous if I saw my friend and her dad getting along. I wished I could have mine back. Or if my friend's dad got mad and yelled, I would tell her at least he was still alive to yell. My friends had no idea how lucky they were to still have their dads in their lives.

Losing a parent at a young age taught me more sympathy toward others than I probably would have had otherwise. I could empathize with them and help give an encouraging word. Communication is a hard element of every relationship that we have. Without it, things crumble. I liked to be the peacekeeper. I wanted everyone happy so I would go out of my way to smile and be cheerful to others. If I saw my friends fighting, I would try to intervene and make peace between them, even if it meant losing their friendship for a while.

Now that I am an adult who has overcome trials and tribulations in my life, I can reflect back and see that my past has led me down the path where I needed to be in life. I still want peace among people. I hate the negative and only want the positive. I've heard the saying "life is not fair" over and over again, but in my reality it is fair. It is what God has chosen to give to each of us. Each day is a breath of fresh new air and I am grateful for it.

How do I sustain this type of thinking?

> *Be strong and courageous. Do not be afraid or terrified because of them, for the Lord your God goes with you; he will never leave you nor forsake you.* (Deuteronomy 31:6)

Finding balance in my life is how I can keep things together. Besides working, being a mom, daughter and friend, I believe in getting involved: involved in charities, communities and church. I don't do it as a favor to anyone but myself. It gives me fulfillment.

I love to start something new that will benefit others. It gives me a thrill and energy shift to start thinking of ways to get it going. That is why I interact so well with others. I like to get other people's ideas. I love to be out with people. I have to socialize. I have to have that interaction.

On the other hand, I love the thrill of giving ideas back to others and having their eyes light up when they realize it can be done and that they are worth it. I love to see people put words into action. Everyone is worth it and everyone has something that needs to be shared with the world in a positive manner.

Something else that gives me balance is getting active. Walking is my favorite form of exercise. I get outside as much as I can during the nice weather and it really is an energy cleanser. I love the starry nights when I'll take my dogs out for a walk and I look up to the heavens and just start talking to the people who have passed before me. I ask for their guidance. I give God the glory for the beautiful day and night.

Before 2014, I would have never been able to say this, but after going to a few retreats and learning more about myself I now say I'm a bold, courageous, loving, vulnerable woman. The word vulnerable is scary to me. Who wants to be vulnerable? I know I didn't in the past, but now I choose to be. It is letting others see a personal side of me I never would have. I never used to cry in public. After my father passed when my mom, my brothers and I sat in church, I would be mortified if my mom cried. I didn't want to see her sad and didn't want people to notice us. I used to constantly watch her to see if she was crying and would put my arm around her if she was.

In our home, my bedroom was downstairs and hers was upstairs. After my father passed, I would lie in bed and listen to her breathe and sometimes snore; so then I knew she was okay. Other nights I heard her cry. Those were the nights I hated. I would cry myself to sleep because I hated to hear it. As the years passed after his death, the crying lessened and the wounds healed. I'm not sure when this happened, but what I have learned about life is that time keeps moving forward. It heals and makes us grow older and wiser. I feel life is worth living with great abundance, and crying is healing and I have embraced that. I let more of my emotions show now than I ever have. The older I get the less I care what people think of my family and me. It is an awesome feeling. Either they love me or hate me; but either way, move over, because life is worth living and I keep moving forward.

I will go out of my way to help others, whether by opening a door, providing a shoulder to cry on, or even talking over a cup of coffee. That is how I feel I can give back. We all have hardships in our lives and just need someone to care for us when it feels as if no one does.

I love the phrase "pay it forward." I'm a big proponent of it. I don't have a lot of extra time or money, but I help in little ways. I donate my time to our local food shelter or help organize a giving Christmas tree. It is what tugs at my heart. What tugs at your heart? Give back and let it help fulfill your soul. Happiness shows because we never know what other people are going through in their daily lives. Everybody is fighting a battle. So, any way we can, we should help them. Even though they might look like they have it all, I have found that they don't.

I used to have a problem dealing with the "now" of life. But I've learned that what I need to do is read my Bible. I received a new Bible in 2013, but to be honest, I hardly read it. That changed in the fall of 2014. I decided that I would read it as often as I could. Sometimes that is every day and other times it is at least once a week. I'm not perfect and life gets in the way, but I do relish the word of the Bible and my daily devotions. Praying is my vigil and my alone time with God. It helps me clear the soul to take on another day.

I always thought I would be scared of solitary activities, so I would keep myself busy in order to avoid it. The thing that I avoided the most is the thing I needed the most. Learning to enjoy alone time has propelled me into a deeper level of thinking and enduring life. I enjoy my time alone. With my dogs by me, I will grab a cup of coffee and I'll sit and read a book. I'll journal. I'll write as much as I can until there is no more coming out of my pen; then I know I am done journaling. Some days have longer entries than others. Spending alone time has propelled me into being able to help others more than ever before. What a weird concept! Something I avoided for years is what is helping me the most to help others. It also aided me in writing this book. Writing has been healing for my soul.

Go forth and bring favor into your life, whatever that is. Find your purpose and ability to help others. When you give to others faithfully, not doing it for what is in it for you, then you will get paid back.

Female business owners are a tough breed. We know how to give back, now let's do it generously. Listen to your heart and follow it. You will be amazed at what God has in store for you if you will just listen to your heart and let it sing a song within you. Spend alone time with yourself and let the word of your most high speak to you. Life is precious and growing older is a privilege reserved for some but not all. Let us rejoice and be glad in it.

CHAPTER 2

I Can Do It My Own Self

My MOTHER likes to tell this story about me: when I was about two years old I wanted to ride a trike by myself and my dad wanted to help me with it. He taught me that the wheels go round and round and how to make the pedals move. Once he taught me that, I kept telling him "I do it my own self, I do it my own self." Then I got on it, started pedaling and off I rode down to the end of the block. My mom and dad couldn't believe it.

My dad used to call me "Little Miss Independent." So as you see, even from my early years, I was very independent. That has continued throughout my life.

During high school, I was good in sports and I had a lot of friends. I played softball, volleyball and basketball. My life revolved around sports. I couldn't wait until the next sporting event came up. I even thought someday I would play professional basketball or volleyball. I loved having big, bodacious dreams.

So with business, as in life, we need to have big, bodacious dreams. But as with anything, these cannot be accomplished without action. We still need to work to get where we want to be. Our lives are always changing.

Since I was the only girl in my family, my two older brothers always used me as their sports partner. I had to play football with them. I had to wrestle with them. I played the night games with them and they hated it when I won. I always had to be on my toes with my brothers around. I had to play defense, as I never knew when they were going to want to use me as their punching bag, wrestling partner or football player. Now, before you start feeling sorry for me, don't think I am 100 percent innocent and didn't provoke it. I didn't start a lot of it, but once I became accustomed to the rivalry it did give me a thrill.

There were those times when I would be laying out on a lounge chair on our patio on a hot summer day, basking in the sun, my boom box playing, enjoying my day. Then all of a sudden, a cold bucket of water would be tipped on me from the roof of our house by my oldest brother. I would scream at him; then it was game on. It was the thrill of adventure that was so fun. He lived for the reaction I would give him.

As I got older, I got smarter. What a concept, huh? Since my older brothers usually had their friends over when they were harassing me I eventually learned not to react, but to give paybacks. I now recognize this as being passive aggressive. So, I would sneak up on them when they were not expecting it and pay back the favor. Smart? Maybe or maybe not, depending on the circumstances. At that point, Mom usually got involved. Then we would get the lecture that it is all fun and games until someone gets hurt.

An example of getting even with my brothers was when my mom would hang out our clothes on the line to dry during the summer. My oldest brother's baseball uniform was hanging out to dry and Mom asked me to bring in the clothes. I brought in everything except his jock strap. That was one thing I would never touch. After I brought in the clothes it was the lone ranger on the clothesline. Little paybacks like that were sweet revenge.

Do you recognize yourself doing this in your business? I do. However, I don't "sneak" up on anyone. I've learned not to react when things go harshly. Through the years I have had my actions cause backlash so I back off and let things simmer before I make a statement. It could be a day, a week, a month or even a year before I say something but I eventually do find myself speaking up about the situation when I find it is appropriate. I love the saying, "Don't ever mistake my silence for ignorance, my calmness for acceptance and my kindness for weakness." This holds very true in both personal and work relationships.

As a female entrepreneur, have you done all of the training you can to stay on top of your game? Because where you lack, there will always be others on your tail waiting to take the lead. Go back to school, take online classes, participate in seminars, put on workshops. Do what you can do to stay on top of things.

I was the first one out of my immediate family to graduate from college. Once I graduated with my Bachelor of Arts in Human Services, I figured I would go out and everybody would want to hire me. I figured I had this college degree and who wasn't going to want to hire me? I figured I would start out making fifty to sixty thousand dollars a year. You know, "the big bucks." Or so I thought. The day I graduated from college was Mother's Day, 1988. The next week I had an interview to be a social worker for the state of South Dakota. Another gal I was graduating with had an interview for the same job. I was so confident that I would get it because of my credentials. But guess what? I didn't. She got it instead. I felt a major letdown. I reasoned with myself that it wasn't a high-paying job so she could have it instead. I started applying for more jobs, and what a mind and ego blow I had when I told my future employers how much I wanted to make. I felt employers were laughing at me. They asked how much experience I had. I said, "Well, none, but your job will give me that experience." Some laughed me out of their businesses.

It was like my goal of getting my dream job was getting crushed, little by little, every time I went for an interview. I figured I had it all going on since I had a college diploma. Then I discovered that once you go out and start applying for jobs, you're not someone every business wants to hire after all. Businesses want to hire you, but you don't have the experience. Yet you can't get the experience unless somebody hires you. It's a vicious cycle.

The same goes for when you own your own business. When you first start running your own business, you think you're going to go out and make the "big bucks" and everybody is going to want to hire you, when in reality, that's not necessarily the case. You know you have the experience and the knowledge to make your business profitable. However, you also have to do some things that can be scary. You have to make your presence known. And people won't hire someone with no experience. You have to brag about yourself and hope you get the clients. If you keep finding that potential clients are asking for the same type of task and you're not sure how to do it, go and learn how. You be will be employable if you do.

The same thing when I got out of college. I was just so determined I would be making big money for the jobs that I wanted, I would go out and I would try to learn how to do those jobs so the businesses would hire me. To learn the skills needed I did volunteer work. I helped out in the community doing the skill I needed to learn. I made it happen.

Alongside my work goal was my personal goal. I wanted the American dream. I wanted a tall, dark and handsome husband, and a house with a white picket fence. I wanted three kids. My best friend Brenda and I would sit out on the front steps of my house and look up to the stars and dream about how awesome our adult lives were going to be. We were going to be "rich" even though we did not articulate what "rich" was. It was just fun to talk about being rich. It was fun to dream and think about our future since we had our entire lives in front of us. I haven't kept up with Brenda since high school, but I sure have fond memories of our time on the front steps dreaming.

While in college I met my son's dad. He was tall, dark and handsome. I thought I had finally met the man with whom I thought I would spend the rest of my life. We graduated at the same time from college. We were off to set the world on fire. Those fun years of sitting out on my front steps looking at the stars and wishing for all of my personal dreams were finally coming true. Or, so I thought.

God had different plans for us. We were married five days after my twenty-first birthday, and we were divorced when I was twenty-four. We separated when I was pregnant with my son due to his infidelity. Cody was born October 22, 1991 and our divorce was final three months later. I was now a single mother wondering how in the world I was going to make it.

When you marry at such a young age, sometimes those ideal dreams are far-fetched, especially when you're just graduating from college. You have student loans and bills and you have to stretch yourself thin in order to work and try and get ahead. In order to come close to the money I wanted to earn, I took on a part-time job while working full-time and being pregnant. It was a difficult situation.

While I was pregnant with my son, I found out his dad was having affairs and I felt vulnerable. I had to realize my worst fear was coming true. Divorce was never in my vocabulary. I never, ever thought I would be divorced. I had been on a newlywed high from our marriage, and getting separated and divorced brought me right back down to ground zero. Slowly, I had to work my way back up again, inch by inch.

Once I'd gone through all that, I realized I had more internal strength then I ever thought possible. "Doing it my own self" became real during this time. I knew my child needed me and I was alone. I loved my baby as soon I as knew I was pregnant. I fought back through the pain and it taught me that even though we are put in these vulnerable positions, we can become stronger. When all you know is to be tough and endure each day, that is what gets you through. When Cody was born, it was the greatest day of my life. My spirits were lifted through this experience. The knowledge that I now had another individual to care for made me bound and determined that no one would stop me from being the best mom I could be.

Even when we're going through tough times, we should be kind to others. I tried doing that with all my friends, family and strangers. My friends were absolutely wonderful to me. Through all of my trials during that time, I never lost my kindness, faithfulness, self-control, smile, and laughter. And God made it possible for me to learn how to forgive. God had blessed me with my beautiful son Cody and I knew if

I wanted to be a better person and mom, I had to forgive Cody's dad. It takes a lot of guts to forgive and it doesn't take away the pain; it takes away the hatred for the other person. It took me five years to fully forgive, but I finally did. My life became so much more enriched and alive once I forgave.

> *But the fruit of the Spirit is love, joy, peace, patience, kindness, goodness, faithfulness, gentleness and self-control. Against such things there is no law.* (Galatians 5:22-23)

Once we're able to forgive in business and in life, it doesn't matter. Business ventures go awry too, but once we're able to forgive, I think the world opens up whole new possibilities for you and you're able to really hone in on those, and on where your strengths and weaknesses are.

I didn't know how to be a mom. Nobody gave me an instruction booklet or anything; especially how to be a *single* mom. I was scared. My mother came and stayed with Cody and me for a couple of days after we got out of the hospital. When she left that Sunday night, I looked out the front screen door and watched her drive away. I had tears in my eyes wondering how I was going to do this. I was cradling Cody in my arms. I looked down at my five-day-old infant wrapped up in his blanket and said, "Well it's just you and me now, kiddo." But I knew we would be okay and that I could draw strength from my mother. Since my dad had died at such an early age, she was a single mom too and she taught me a lot. She taught me much of the strength and endurance I needed to be that single mom. She told me all the time how proud she was of me for being such a good mom for my son. For me there is no greater joy than being Cody's mom.

You just have to keep plugging forward no matter what life brings you in business and in your personal life. You can't let that fear, hatred and anger get you down. If you do, you will remain paralyzed.

I don't like people feeling sorry for me. I realized through the divorce that people felt sorry for me. I needed the support but not the sympathy. It also propelled me to become a better person and mother. I wanted to show the world I was better than my circumstances. And no matter what life threw at me, I always had a smile on my face. I learned to laugh through the pain.

Being a single mom meant I was financially strapped. I had a wonderful job that I loved but the pay was less than desirable. Actually, it was poverty level. I had to learn to juggle finances, especially since I still had bills from the divorce. It did teach me how to have a good budget and that we don't always need all the things we have, in life, such as cable television, a lot of furniture, etc. Those are just wants. The needs are food on the table and transportation to work. I learned how to live frugally. Did I want more? Absolutely. Was I striving for more? You bet. But until that time when I had more to spend, my most important job was caring for Cody and surviving. And that's what I did.

I didn't receive child support for a full year after Cody's birth. His dad fought me through the courts on it, but I eventually won the battle. When the child support started coming in regularly it did help the financial burden. I drove a Geo Metro for ten years and it cost me ten dollars to fill it up with gas, so I had no problem driving it. In fact, it was the best little car I've ever had. My mom called my Geo my "little snowplow" because it went through snow like a snowplow. I never got stuck. Living frugally really taught me to evaluate my circumstances.

I was awarded a state job when Cody was four weeks old. I started it when he was six weeks old. With this position I could move to different states with the same job. When Cody was two and a half, I decided it was time to move out of South Dakota. There were employment ads up on our walls at work. The state of Nevada paid substantially more than South Dakota did. I visited Nevada and decided that was where my life was going to take us. The job was in Carson City and the climate was so much better than South Dakota's. I was ready for a break from winter. It was a scary thought to move on my own without a spouse. But I was determined to make it work.

I knew I needed to move out of South Dakota to start my life over again. Some people were negative and some were positive about the move. I listened to the positive people and tuned out the negative ones. I knew this was the right decision for my son and me. The negative people could not believe I would leave the security of my life and family to pursue a better job. They felt it was wrong to move my two- and-a-half-year-old son away from his family. The positive people said, "Go for it!" Cody wasn't in school yet and I was young, so now was time to do it. I loved the way they thought! It drove me. While visiting Nevada I checked out daycare facilities, apartments, and my job. I got everything lined up and I was ready for the move.

What have you done that you were determined to make work and for which you have no regrets? Starting your own business? Making a move like I did? Pushing through the negativity and following the positive is what works.

The goodbyes were hard at home but I was so intent on being successful that I couldn't look back. My Geo was packed solid. I had a girlfriend drive out to Nevada with me. We were in the front two seats and Cody was strapped in his car seat in the back, among all of our belongings. I was twenty-six years old when we left and turned twenty-seven on our trip. It was rewarding because once we got there, I knew I could accomplish anything. I was certain this was a great decision.

That decision to move was one of the best things I've ever done. We were so much better off financially. But more importantly, I learned I had it in me to take a risk and go out on my own. I felt such a wonderful sense of personal accomplishment.

For my own growth - my internal, spiritual and mental well-being - I had to venture out. I just knew I would stagnate if I stayed where I was. Venturing out that way and doing it myself enabled me to grow. I became a better person and a better mother because I didn't have anybody to rely on except myself.

Starting a business is a big leap of faith. Going alone is a struggle sometimes, because now you are the boss. No more water cooler talk. My advice is to find a confidant to talk with and from whom you can get input. Such people will be invaluable to you as time goes on. Some of my best confidants were my clients. They taught me so much about how to keep on going after struggles. They were my inspiration and determination.

When venturing out on my own, I never worried if I was going to get sick. I never worried if my car was going to break down. I didn't think about such things. I just did what I had to do. I was young and a spontaneous person. Though I had it planned out, and I learned that sometimes you just have to go for it. Even if something bad happens, everything will work out. When you follow God's plan for your life it all seems to work out.

Overcoming that fear of taking action brings confidence. That is how I felt about moving. Now that I had taken the leap of faith and moved from one state to another, I knew I could move again if better opportunities came available.

One of the many benefits of working for state government was they were always very accommodating with schedules. They knew I was a single mom and that my child came first. My employers went out of their way to make sure my schedule coordinated with theirs. I felt truly blessed.

You have to learn very good time and financial management skills when working full-time, having your baby in daycare and trying to live a life. Just completing your daily tasks of getting up, getting him to daycare and working can be a big accomplishment.

But I liked to do other things too. I am not a stay-at-home-type of person. I love to get out and do things. I am also a big fan of fitness but at the time could not afford a gym membership. With South Dakota winters as cold as they are, I liked to work out in the comfort of a warm gym; so I got creative. Since I couldn't be a paying member, I would work at the gym's daycare during my lunch hour so my membership would be free. At night, I would go work out while he went to the gym's daycare.

I did that a lot through Cody's younger years. I would get creative so I could afford the things I wanted and needed. At one point I also used to work part-time at his daycare in the mornings before I went to work. This way my daycare costs were less expensive and I had more in my paycheck at the end of the day.

I was always thinking ahead so I could plan out my time and life accordingly. My time was valuable, as is everyone else's. Sunday nights were when I would sit down and plan out my week. For a spontaneous person like myself that was really hard! I'm not a list person. I go with the flow and whatever happens, happens. This would drive some people crazy, but this is how I roll. I would check Cody's daycare schedule to map out his week, and I knew my work and fitness schedule, so everything coordinated. And if things changed I wouldn't get upset; we would just readjust our schedules and roll with it.

Keeping organized during busy and hectic times was a bit more of a challenge. When schedules collide (and they do), start making a priority list. I would sit on Sunday nights and list out things I needed to accomplish both at work and at home.

What happened when Cody got sick? I would immediately take off work and go get him. But what happens when there is a fire at the daycare your son goes to? That happened to Cody.

He went to an in-home daycare in Nevada. One night in November, I went to pick him up. It was about 5:30 pm, it was dark and the house was at the end of a cul-de-sac. As I drove up something was definitely different about the house. I couldn't go too far into the cul-de-sac before I had to stop. I stared at the garage and realized something was horribly wrong. It was all black from smoke. My heart sank and I started shaking. Just then the daycare provider ran up to my car with Cody in her arms. I jumped out and grabbed for Cody. He had his winter coat on and it smelled like smoke. I still remember that smell. He was crying and my daycare lady was frantic. She had tried calling me but I never got the call at work. I didn't have a cell phone then. She had grabbed her piece of paper with our information on it and somehow the number to my work was not right. I never even thought to verify it with her once she had our information. I never made that mistake again. The fire had started three hours before I got there. I had no idea. Thankfully no one was hurt in the fire and she and her helper got all of the children out safely. I never hugged Cody as tight as I did right then.

While the daycare provider was trying to find shelter and a new home for herself and her family, I had to come up with a new daycare provider and quickly. I searched the phone books and asked people. I took the next day off of work so I could locate one. The lady who had the fire had a friend who said she would take some of the children. After interviewing her the next day, I decided she would be a good fit. That is how quickly things can change.

Even though I was a single mom and even though I had to do a lot of things myself, I had wonderful friends and family on whom I could rely if I needed. Sometimes it's not always good to rely on yourself, and I learned that as a single mom; that even though my philosophy was "I can do it my own self," I couldn't actually do it all myself. I needed to rely on other people to help me. After the fire, I came to fully realize how much I had to have other people in my life. I needed their help and guidance. Friends and other people are not likely to give you money but they will give you the gift of themselves. This is more valuable than money.

Once you allow people to help you, I find they are often willing to go out of their way. I found that a lot being a single parent, especially if I told them my situation. I didn't want anybody to feel sorry for me, but sometimes I just had to stress that I was a single parent and needed help. It was hard for me to give up that independence in a way, but it was fulfilling knowing I wasn't alone. The more you tell people, the more they're willing to help. Another advantage is the ability to network. Friends and acquaintances know people you don't. They can refer you to others who might be able to meet your needs. Be open, be interactive; see how many new people you can meet.

This applies to business as well. If you're out there and you're struggling, ask for help. When I was trying to learn other skills in my business I was always asking for help, or I was asking where I could go to find that help. Just like I did with coordinating my responsibilities as a single mom. I had to ask people where I could go for help or if they could help me. It was not always my family.

I really found out who my true friends were and how wonderful my family was. I knew I could rely on them when I needed help, especially when I was three states away from my family. I made new friends who knew people in the state where I now lived. Once you know you can rely on people, there's no greater assurance and greater peace.

This works as well for business, especially when you're a solo entrepreneur. If you know there are people you can rely on, go to them. Search them out and have them help you because it really will make a difference in your business and in your life. It will give you more peace and comfort knowing you can rely on those people to help.

To stay motivated, you have to find things that are going to wake you up and shake you. I get bored easily. Something new and exciting energizes me. The more I thought about moving and making more money, the more excited I became. It drove me to search out my new location, find daycare and a place to live. I researched the cost of living and calculated my finances. I wasn't stressed; I was driven.

With anything different you try, there are always positive and negative factors that go with it. In reality, there were a lot of things and ideas I said no to. I said yes to many things, but I said no more often. A lot of times if it didn't feel right in my gut, I didn't do it. I learned the hard way if my gut said no and I did it anyway, bad consequences soon followed.

What is your gut telling you to do? There is a difference between fear of the unknown and your gut downright telling you no. When the answer is no, it actually feels like someone punching me and I feel down about the decision or very indecisive. What is your gut saying?

Whatever the idea or thought process is, ask yourself, "Does this excite or deflate me?" Do you wake up in the middle of the night and have thoughts running through your head? If so, write them down. A lot of times when you wake up in the morning you're not going to remember what you thought of during the night. So write them down or record them. If the thought excites you, then pursue it. If it doesn't excite you, then throw it away and try something different. A lot of my ideas come when I am in the shower. I won't be thinking of anything else and then all of a sudden something pops into my head. Once I am out of the shower, I write it down.

What excites me is something new that will produce income. I also think of ideas about how to help others. I have friends who lost their only child to a car accident when she was eight years old. Shortly after her death, I was in the shower and thought of creating a nonprofit in her memory. I have not acted upon this idea. But it still remains clear in my memory.

While I love to think and act upon new ideas the one thing I have a hard time with is doing the mundane work once the idea or business is up and running. I know that about myself. I don't like it, but it's something I have to do. I have to stay committed to what I'm doing. Staying committed is seeing it through the long haul. I always want to skip ahead to the good times. In life we have to go through the hard times to get to and enjoy the good times.

I always want to move on to the next new and exciting thing. I want to just move on to the next, and to the next, and to the next. But, I learned that if I kept moving on to the next big thing I wasn't able to let the last good thing catch me. After a while, I learned how to sit and be still. I learned to listen to myself and work and be committed to the job I had.

Once I learned to do that, my business actually grew. To try to get motivated and try to stay on top of things, determine what excites you? What's deep down in your gut that excites you? If the job you're doing now doesn't thrill you, then I would certainly look for something else. Life is too short to not be in something that you enjoy or something that makes life worth living for you.

Find something that you love. Do you like to write? Do you like to read? If you do, maybe during those times that you need motivation, read more or do more artwork; whatever it is that you like to do. Sometimes we just have to take a step back and do these things in order for us to gain more mileage and more power in our businesses.

If you want to start your own business or if you are in your own business, keep going. Keep going after it, because if it's something that you're passionate about, you shouldn't stop. I've learned the hard way; I'll start doing something and then I'll stop and move on to something else. But if you're passionate about something, keep going. Time is going to work for you and be on your side if you keep after your dream. If you are finding it difficult, look for somebody else to help you. People will support you but it will be up to you to get it going. Remember, "Do it my own self." You are worth it and can do it. That's going to be invaluable. Just go after what you want in life and you'll never regret it.

CHAPTER 3
The Move to Colorado

THE SUMMER before my fourth grade in elementary school, my cousins from Colorado came to visit. With the excitement of a little girl, I remember thinking, *I can't wait till they get here!* I remember counting down the days, then the hours, till they arrived. I hadn't seen them in a couple of years so it was exciting to see the "Colorado" cousins. When they did finally arrive, they talked about the mountains and how beautiful they were. How they loved living in Colorado and wanted us to come out for a visit soon. I begged my parents and their words were, "Someday we will." My parents weren't into long family vacations. We took small vacations, going to visit relatives who didn't live beyond a four-hour trip, and Colorado didn't fit into that category. The small trips were wonderful as I got to know my other relatives well that way. We were a close-knit family and I loved that. But I wanted more. I remember thinking, *Someday I'm going to live in Colorado,* because that just sounded absolutely beautiful to me.

When John Denver released his song "Rocky Mountain High" on the radio, I would listen to it intently and sing along with it at the top of my voice. Eventually my parents got the record, so I played it over and over and over again. My brothers would say, "Turn that off already. We're tired of hearing it." I just knew back then that someday I was going to live in Denver, Colorado.

I never outgrew that dream. As I got into high school and eventually adulthood I still had that dream. Have you ever wanted a dream so bad that you knew it would eventually happen? When I was twenty-one, I took a trip to Colorado and visited my aunt, uncle and cousins. That visit confirmed for me that I would live there.

While living and working in Nevada I realized that wasn't the place for Cody and me. I was having a lot of fun with the people I had met there, but it didn't feel like home. The thought of continuing to live in a state where gambling was the most prominent influence for tourists didn't interest me. So the hunt was on for a new job and possibly a new state. Colorado wasn't hiring at that time. So maybe it was time to move a little closer to home. The thought of going back to South Dakota was of no interest to me at that time. So I contacted the state of Iowa and that was where my next job was taking us. Again we packed up our belongings from Nevada and made the long trek to Iowa. This time there were no friends to help make the move with me. Friends helped pack my little Geo Metro and off Cody and I headed to the state of Iowa.

I was a year into working in Iowa when I decided to pursue the state of Colorado again for a job. I went for a visit and toured the job location, and was awestruck again by the mountains and the climate. My heart skipped a beat when I saw those mountains. There were some friends from my past who lived there and some of my relatives were still there. I was bound and determined that I would not give up until I had that job. I knew the state had a hiring freeze on and the superiors could not tell me how long it would last because they did not know. I wrote down my goal of calling the office at least once every one to two months. I didn't give up and that persistence finally paid off.

Then one day out of the blue, in May 1997, I came home from work, and there was a message on my answering machine. They asked me to call them back. I just knew it was a job offer. My fingers and body were shaking when I was dialing the phone to call them back. When the gal answered on the other line she asked me, "When can you start?" I was jumping up and down while talking on the phone with her. I'm not sure she realized that, but I was. I was so ecstatic that I was screaming because the dream was finally coming to fruition. Cody was five years old at the time and started crying because he wasn't sure what was going on and had never heard me that ecstatic before. I told him our dreams were coming true and we were moving to the great state of Colorado!

I went back to work the next day and ironically a fellow coworker said jokingly, "When is that big move to Colorado coming?"

I looked him in the eyes and said, "June 1st, in three weeks." His mouth dropped to the floor.

He said, "What? Are you kidding me?"

"Yeah, June 1st of this year." I had been talking about the move to Colorado for over six months. So they knew I wanted that job. They all gave me a hug, wished me well, and I turned in my two weeks' notice. I started my job out in Denver on June 9th. My dream was alive and I was living it! It was the best thing I've ever done.

If you're trying to pursue your dreams and goals, don't give up on them. Keep after them. You will have setbacks. Those setbacks are there to make you determined to finish your goal. Just realize they are only setbacks. You have to keep pursuing forward. I just can't stress that enough, because I had said, "They have a hiring freeze and they don't know how long it's going to be. It could be two years; it could be five years. It could be one year; it could be six months. Who knows?" But I didn't give up. I wanted my name on their radar so I kept pursuing them until they finally offered me the position.

Cody started kindergarten in Colorado in August 1997. I was scared. My baby boy was going off to school and we were in a big new city, in new school, and as of then he had no friends. However, my son shines like I do when we converse and mingle with others. He made friends the first day he went to school. He got wonderful friends. Like with our move to Colorado, we have to place our trust in God and know it will work out. No matter what your circumstances, things usually fall into place. Then, if something doesn't work one way, you find another way to make it work. One of my favorite sayings is, "If you can't go in the front door, go in the back door."

Once Cody was in school I remember thinking one day, *I'm just going to take off work early, and I'm going to go pick him up from school. We're just going to have a fun afternoon.* He was so surprised to see me picking him up from school. He had the biggest grin on his face. He and I went rollerblading that afternoon then out for supper.

At supper he looked at me and said, "Mom, guess what? I've got a girlfriend." And in a kindergarten kind of way, he giggled sheepishly. I just grinned from ear to ear, because then I knew we were at the right place, because he had all these friends now, and supposedly in kindergarten, his first girlfriend.

Life was great. It really became balanced once we figured out our schedules. Learning a new city, especially a city as big as Denver, can be a lot of work and very daunting. To overcome the greatness of a big city I chose to focus on the little area where we lived. That's what I recommend for people in business too. Focus on the small, and then grow bigger. If I had focused on the big city of Denver, I might have had an anxiety attack just trying to learn all of the areas. I looked at maps, talked to people, and asked my co-workers. My 1995 Geo Metro got a lot of miles put onto it because we were out driving around a lot learning the area.

The job that I had was very flexible and family friendly. As a single mom, I needed that. I could work variable shifts and take time for Cody's school functions. My mom taught me right from when Cody was born, "I raised my kids, now you have to raise yours." I didn't like to bother people with picking up my son when he was my responsibility. Although, I knew people would help if needed, since I had wonderful friends and family. The best thing I did was take time for Cody and hang out with him. Instinctively, I knew someday he was going to grow up and the early days would be gone. It is the same thing with your business. If you have work and family life, take time for that family, take time for those kids. They need you. Work around your schedule, so you make time for your family. You'll never get that time back with your kids.

Since I couldn't be at home with him when he was little, I was so thankful for a job where I could have a flexible schedule. Cody and I had a lot of fun. We would go to go kart parks, kids play areas, go hiking and exploring, anything that we could do together. We would go up to the mountains almost every weekend for about the first six months we lived there. I cherish those memories.

One month after moving to Denver, I decided to purchase my first cell phone. I was excited and scared. I didn't want the extra payment but living in a big city, I wanted the security of knowing I could call someone if something ever was to happen. Cell phones were just becoming popular but not everyone had them yet. So it was a big step to put forth the effort to purchase it. The next great thing that happened is that we found a mall! Window shopping used to be therapeutic for me. I couldn't spend money, but I could certainly walk around the mall and dream about when I did have money and what I would buy. Driving down I-25 in Denver, Cody asked to call his grandma. With the cell phone, which was almost bigger than his hand, he called his grandma and excitedly proclaimed, "Grandma we got a new cell phone AND found the mall! It's been a GREAT day!"

As long as the focus was on the small areas in our neighborhood it was okay. As I got to know more people at work and felt more comfortable driving around the area, expansion started happening. A friend from South Dakota came to visit us a few weeks after we moved to Colorado. She said, "Do you think we could go to Colorado Springs?"

I said, "Sure, might as well try it." So, off on the adventure we went. What a freeing feeling we had after we conquered that quest. Eventually we were going to downtown Denver and driving up in the mountains like we were old pros.

In business as well, you should always start small. Starting big in business means a lot of money and more room for failure at the beginning. When first beginning your business just focus on the small things that you need. As time goes on and you feel more comfortable, start expanding. Do more marketing; go out and meet more people. Hand out your business cards everywhere you go. Brag up your business. Taking one step at a time leads to success rather than failure. If you don't, if you get too big too fast, you're going to fall.

I consider those years moving from state-to-state my formative years. Even though I was an adult with a small child, I learned a lot. Each goodbye is a learning process and a new beginning for something better in your life. I learned what my strengths and weaknesses were.

My strength is meeting people. I am very good at meeting and talking to people. Turn your strength into a goldmine. But also figure out your weakness. At that time my weakness was not wanting to go do activities or go to social events alone. The thought of going alone and walking in alone made me feel uncomfortable; awkward actually. It felt like everyone was staring at me and feeling sorry for the poor pitiful single mom. Now, I knew that probably wasn't true but that is how I felt. Ever feel that way? Some days it took every ounce of energy I had to go to an event but I made myself do it. I would talk to myself in front of my mirror and make a game of it. My goal would be to go out and meet at least two new people. Why? I knew my strength. I knew if I did I was going to meet people. The more people you meet and know, the more opportunities can come your way. People know people who you don't. It's a great way to connect and network. Your weakness can turn into a strength. Something I didn't want to do actually turned into a strength.

I met a good friend at work. We started the same day and we explored the city and mountains together. The state kept hiring on more people so it was fun getting to know the new employees and I didn't feel as alone. I took some of the new hires under my wing and showed them the city.

When you make a move it can be scary. Having someone to guide you through it can help. That's what I encourage you as a business owner to do. Once you know your specific industry or business, if you know other people trying to get in the business or get into a similar business, show them the ropes. What you do to help other people, the kindness you can show other people will come back to you three- and four- and tenfold. It's just a miracle how that can happen. If you believe, as I believe in God, He can get back to us what we give out.

Two months after I moved to Colorado, I turned thirty. I finally realized that dreams can come true. I pursued my dream of moving to there and finally made it. That was probably the first time I had actually set a goal for myself and accomplished it. That really put a new perspective on my life in terms of how to push forward and just keep going. People would tell me they were inspired by me. I told them if I could do it, anyone could. I heard this saying once: "If you want to see God move, make a move."

I've always heard tenacity is a virtue. I learned this through my moves. It also holds true in business. There are days when you're going to feel like you want to give up. There have been plenty of days and weeks when I wanted to give up. Don't quit! I didn't quit and just knew each step was getting closer to the goal. Each step may get harder, but don't ever stop, because the view at the top is beautiful. I have that saying saved on my laptop as my background picture. I read it every day, several times a day.

There will be times when you don't get the client or the money isn't flowing in the way you want. When these events happen, rearrange your thinking and marketing. Get creative. Make changes. But don't ever quit. Keep at it. Write down your goals, write down what you want to be in three months, six months, nine months, and a year. What is it that you wanted when you started your business? That dream and goal should become your tenacity.

You want a six-figure income? Break down the steps that are going to get you where you're going to make that six-figure income. The most important step is the first step. Soon, you're going to be an expert in your field, and people are going to come begging to hire you.

Just always be aware of your behavior, always be aware of your attitude, always be aware of how you're treating other people. Your attitude toward others will make or break your business. People are going to want to do business with you because they like you. What you have to offer will interest them; but if they don't like you, they will go to someone they do like. Always watch your behavior, and be mindful of how you treat other people. Kindness goes a long way.

CHAPTER 4
Meeting Jim

BEING A single mom can be lonely. I would dream of having a wonderful man by my side. I dreamt of what my future husband would look like. Tall, dark and handsome? Muscles? Yes, I definitely wanted muscles and blond would be good too. It was fun sketching out the man in my dreams. Would it be somebody with children? Would it be somebody who maybe has been married once or twice, but without kids? But the most important question was, would he be willing to call my son his son and love us unconditionally?

Dating was a power struggle for me. I dated some while Cody was young and he was pretty outspoken and protective of his mom. If he didn't like the guy I was dating, he let me know right away: "No way mom, not this guy."

My friend, Faith, works for the city of Greenwood Village, Colorado, and she invited me to the city's annual Christmas event. There were rides and games going on while Christmas music was playing. While walking around, we came up to one table that was a vendor booth. A good-looking gentleman was working there.

He introduced himself as Jim. Faith and I introduced ourselves as well.

As we walked away, I said to Faith, "If you ever find out that man is single, you let me know."

She said, "Okay, I will." We just laughed it off and kept walking around the event.

That Christmas event we attended was in December 1999. Remember the big hype back in 1999 that the world was going to end and all of the computers were going to crash? I wasn't worried. I was too busy to worry. But for some reason I just knew the year 2000 was going to be great. I couldn't explain; I just knew.

It was the beginning of April 2000 when I received a phone call from Faith. She never called me at work so at first I was concerned. She asked me if I was sitting down. I asked what was going on? She said asked again if I was sitting down. I said, "Yeah, I'm at work. Why? What's going on?"

She said, "Well, I gave that one man your number." I about fell over because she knew better than to give out my number to anybody.

I asked, "Who the heck did you give my phone number to?"

She answered, "That guy. That Jim guy you met at Greenwood Village Days." I had absolutely no recollection of who he was. She continued, "Don't you remember, you said, if you ever find out he's single, let me know." I was racking my brain because it had been four or five months since then. It took me the rest of the day to really remember who he was.

I said, "Oh my gosh. Okay, dating right now is like the last thing I wanted to do. I know I said that, but I don't know. I just don't know."

She said, "Well, too late. I gave him your home number. He's going to be calling you. I told him you're going to be home on Tuesday night so you had better be home Tuesday night.

"All right, fine," is all I said.

I'll be honest, I paced the floor that night wondering if he was going to call. Every time the phone rang, I checked caller ID. Then it happened. At 7:05 pm, the phone rang. The caller ID showed his name and number. My heart felt like it skipped a beat. Do I answer it? I let it ring three times before I answered. He introduced himself and he was sweet and polite on the phone. A perfect gentleman.

We decided to meet for a lunch date. We picked that Friday. When the day came, I was so nervous. I was in the bathroom almost all morning. We were meeting at 11:30 and I thought, *Okay, fine, well. It's just lunch. Just go, eat, and leave. That's all you've got to do. You just make some chit chat with him and go on your way.* Then I thought, *No, I'm not going. I'm going to call.* I did this tug of war back and forth all morning long. The closer it got, the more scared I got.

Faith called me. She asked if I was ready to go. I said, "Nope. I'm not going. This is too much. I don't want to go."

She told me, "Oh, you're going. I don't care if I've got to come over and get you. You're going. You're the one who told me, if you ever find out that man is single, and *I* found out he was single for you, so you're going."

I thought, *Oh gosh. Okay, well, here we go.* I said, "Well, I'm in the bathroom. I'm scared. I don't want to go."

"You are going," she stated emphatically.

I did go. We met for lunch. He was already there waiting for me. We had the best time. There was no stress whatsoever. It was like I was talking to somebody I'd known for a long time. He asked a lot of questions about Cody. He had never been married and he had no kids. He was ten years older than I was, but he was taking a big interest in me.

Changes can be scary and so can doing something new. When you are trying to integrate change into your life and try something new, feelings can take over. You want something so badly but when it comes to you, sometimes you overlook it because it isn't what you expected. It comes in different shapes. Open your mind and your environment to something new and see how it can change you.

Being a single mom I didn't put a lot of trust into the dating scene. I guess I wanted somebody who took an interest in my son. Jim was asking a lot of questions. He seemed genuine. That's the only way I can explain it. He was sincere. He was a gentleman. He was good-looking. Good-looking, blonde, with muscles.

After we had dated about a month, he asked me if I minded if he met Cody. I said, "Well, okay. I'm starting to feel more comfortable with you. I think that would be okay." Jim suggested we meet at a rec center and go swimming or maybe play racquetball.

I went home and asked Cody what he thought and he agreed he would go. I told him, "If you don't like him then I won't continue seeing him." He was good with that idea.

Jim had a stepdad who raised him from the age of ten and whom he considered his dad. He knew what it was like to have a stepdad around the same age Cody was at the time. I thought, *Okay, well there's something to this guy. Maybe, just maybe.*

Cody fell in love with him. We started having fun together. We played sports together. We were just having a really good time. It was amazing how one person, one man, could come into our lives and make a big difference.

Business can be like that. Some days you might feel like hanging it all up. I know I did a lot. Some days it felt like it wasn't worth it. Then, when that right client comes along, you feel like you could dance in the rain again. You feel like no one can stop you. It's awesome.

Cody told me he felt like we could be a family again. I reassured him that he and I would be family, no matter what. But, he let me know that if Jim continued to be around, maybe we could be a bigger family.

For his part, Jim assured me he adored Cody and wanted to be a part of his life. I had decided to take things one day at a time not rush anything. That's exactly what we did. We continued to have fun playing sports and continuing to enjoy each other's company.

Keep a positive attitude when the right person hasn't come along yet; you just need patience. Apply this to business too, when you're waiting for that perfect client, or you're waiting for that right person to come in. Maybe you need help with your business. Maybe you need an accountant. Maybe you need an attorney. Practice patience.

That's often the hardest thing for most people, especially entrepreneurs, because most hate becoming stagnant. But we have to practice patience. With my virtual assistance work, I wanted clients badly. I would practically beg, steal, and borrow for them. I would take on clients I didn't like doing work for. I did it so I could get the experience.

You also need to be patient with yourself and stay positive. Learn new skills while you're waiting. Pray about it. Write out your goals and intentions. Trust that the right clients are going to come along.

It helps to believe in God or that higher power, knowing that he's at work with you and will bring the right people into your life. Following Christ is a big aspect of my life. I just couldn't wait to wake up in the morning and go after my business. I knew then that since I was going after it full force, God would supply what I needed.

It was the biggest blessing in my life just knowing that God was on my side and he was going to be sending me the right clients. Sure enough, it happened. It took some time. It didn't happen overnight. It took patience. It took trust.

Opening up a business is frightening. There is that fear about what happens if a mistake is made. And if a previous business has failed, there is the fear of trusting that things will work out this time.

I decided to trust falling in love again. In business too, you have to believe that the customers are going to come into your life. They're waiting for you. But you have to search them out. Find your niche market and go after it.

Like trusting falling in love, you have to trust yourself enough to go after your target customers. It's probably going to be through referrals because that's where most of mine came from. After I got my first few clients, in about six months to a year, I didn't have to do any more advertising. It was all referral-based. I loved every one of them.

There were a few I could have done without, but I still loved them. I loved them enough to know that I could do their work for them. If I couldn't do the work for them, I would refer them on to other people.

Being authentic is being yourself. You can't give a false image of yourself to your clients because if you do, they are never going to stay around. Just like Jim was authentic with Cody. He just came out and said, "I'm not going to shower this kid with gifts, and I'm not going to shower you with gifts either. That's not who I am. This is who I am. I'm Jim. This is what I do." You have to do the same thing for your clients. You have to be that authentic.

Jim went on vacation a month after we first started dating. He had only met Cody once before he left. He actually called me to tell me about this roller coaster ride, because he was ecstatic about it. He wanted to tell Cody about it because he knew Cody loved roller coasters, too. To think that this man who we hardly knew wanted to tell my son about a roller coaster ride gave me wonderful chills that he was thinking of us in this way. That was his gift to us. Cody wasn't home at the time, so I said I would tell him when he got home. I had never had anybody call me while on vacation.

If you learn to be positive and have patience, that will make you an authentic person who people are going to be able to love and trust. Once they love and trust you, they will give you as much work or as much love as you need and deserve. The more you can be positive and patient, the more authentic you become, the more clients you attract, and the more people you attract in your life for the better.

CHAPTER 5
The Proposal and Our Wedding

Jim and I had been dating for about four months when he asked me to take our first camping trip together. I'll be the first to tell you, I don't like camping or sleeping in a tent. I don't like being out in the elements. He understood that but he really enjoyed camping. He told me that when we first met. He had camped a lot as an adult and some as a child. I had only been camping a time or two and was not a fan. After thinking about it for a while, I answered, "Sure, as long as there's a camper."

He said, "No, unfortunately, we have to sleep in a tent, and we have to sleep on the ground." *What?* It was the exact thing I hated to do and he was asking me to do it. I was not a happy girl. To be honest I probably pouted for a little while because I really didn't want to go and he really did want to go.

Sometimes in business, things come our way that we don't really like or don't want to do. That's when we have to assess the situation. It's best to overcome our fears and try something new for the sake of our businesses and also for the sake of our relationships.

I was trying to be a supportive girlfriend and good mother because Cody had not been camping much. So for the sake of Cody and Jim, I agreed to try it. I wanted those two to be happy. They had such a strong connection and I knew that it would strengthen the relationship between the three of us. Trying something with a new and different person can really change a situation. Once the weekend got closer, I was actually looking forward to going since Jim and Cody were so excited about it.

The first weekend of August, we decided to venture out to Burlington, Colorado, where there was a small lake. Jim and his parents used to go there all the time and he had fond memories. He was an avid skier and could slalom ski. He bragged about his mom being able to do the same thing.

Up to this point I had never met his mom. Jim had confided in me that she was an alcoholic. While he was young, he had bad memories of things his mom had done and said, but overall, he still loved her. Deep down in his heart he had learned to forgive her. He learned to cope with her drinking through counseling and family therapy. He was embarrassed by her and didn't want me to meet her yet. However, she heard we were going to the lake and wanted to join us. I still remember the look on Jim's face when he sheepishly asked me if I minded if she came along. Since I'm a person who loves to meet others I said, "Sure. That would be great."

The weekend came for the big camping trip. My good friend was getting married the same Saturday so I packed up the boys and sent them on their way. I stayed back in Denver for half a day so I could attend the wedding. Once Jim and Cody took off they stopped to pick up Jim's mom. After the wedding, I ventured out on the two-hour trip to Burlington. Jim and I had cell phones but back then the cell service wasn't as good. Once I got to Burlington, a big storm kept me in the town; it took me about an hour to get through on my cellphone to get to Jim.

When Jim came to pick me up he was very distraught, which was something I had never seen from him before. His facial expression was one of despair. Jim was a pretty low-key type of guy. He was slow to anger and never swore. He said, "We have a problem." I asked him what it was and he said, "My mother's drunk."

When we planned this trip, my best friend, Faith, her two kids, and significant other decided to join us. Jim's mom was out there drunk with all the kids and our friends and he was deeply embarrassed. He didn't know what to do. I had never met Evelyn before, and he didn't want me to meet her in this fashion. I said, "It's okay. Let's just go out there, and I will meet her, and we'll just deal with it. I mean, that's just how we have to do it, is deal with it."

When the unexpected happens in business dealings, it's best to deal with things head on, even if they're unpleasant. Instead of procrastinating about the situation, just address it right away.

That was how I felt about this situation. May as well deal with it head on. I was okay with it. Once we got out to the campground and met Evelyn, I assessed the situation. The kids were fine. They were off playing at the playground. Evelyn was in her tent needing to take a nap. Jim had taken his dad's boat on this trip. Unfortunately, it didn't start once he put it in the water. The storm had torn Evelyn's tent apart but thankfully Jim and Faith's boyfriend could put it back together. Evelyn wasn't any bigger than about 110 pounds. So when the storm hit, I was told she was holding onto her tent so she wouldn't blow away. Faith said it wasn't funny but yet it was. Evelyn laughed about it later too.

The one thing I always ask is where the bathrooms and showers are when I'm camping. One of my fears is waking up in the middle of the night, having to use the bathroom, and not knowing where it is. Then having to walk to a bathroom didn't please me either. Jim was very good about showing me where everything was, and he said, "You know, unfortunately, in these types of showers, there could be more than one person in the shower with you. There are no separate showers." All I thought was, *Ugh. What have I gotten myself into?*

After Jim showed me where the showers were, he and I and the three kids were walking back to our tents. The kids were laughing and joking around with each other. Jim could tell I wasn't having a very good time. He knew I was kind of upset about the whole situation but I was trying to make the best of it. He was trying to say good things to lighten the mood. Cody, who was eight years old at the time, decided he would pipe in. Without warning, he said out loud with everything an eight-year-old can muster, "Jim, if you asked my mom to marry her, she would say yes."

I about fell over. My eyes got really big, and Jim said, "Oh, really? She would, huh?" Then Cody said, "Yep, she would. Just ask her."

I was so embarrassed. My face was beet red. I was looking down. I wanted to crawl into a hole. I'd only known Jim for four months. I didn't know if I wanted to marry him or not. Just the week before was when we told each other we loved one another. I looked at Cody in total shock with a look of *when I get you alone you are in so much trouble* that only a mom can give her child. The can of beans had been opened; how do you address something like that? I had never mentioned to Cody that I would marry Jim. But kids are great that way. They have a better perception than we do. He knew what his mom wanted and needed.

I wasn't sure what to say to Jim. Did that scare him? Was he happy about it? Did he even care? I needed to let him know he could call off the relationship if he wanted to. That would be my out. Put the pressure back on him so I didn't have to be so bewildered. So I said to Jim, "It's already been an interesting weekend meeting your mom, the storm, and then my son saying that, so if you want to run for the hills, I'm fine with it. I totally would understand. You don't have to put up with this."

Instead of that, he turned around and grabbed my hand, and he said, "Absolutely not." You have helped me with my mom and her troubles this weekend, and I just think it was cute what Cody said."

I couldn't and wouldn't look at him. I hung my head and Jim put his fingers underneath my chin and with a gentle nudge, tilted my head up. He said, "It's okay. Let's just keep walking."

I don't know if I've ever been that embarrassed, but yet I was so tickled that Cody was speaking his mind. To know he thought that much of Jim was a wonderful tribute to the type of person Jim was. Although I was in shock, it really was fun to see the look on Cody's face when he saw our expressions. Cody's eyes got big and his mouth opened with a wide smile. It was a look I'll never forget. The fact that Jim didn't say no was a strong point for him.

The weekend was like a comedy of errors. When that happens, we just have to laugh about it, shake it off and keep moving forward; and that was what we were doing. What could have been a bad weekend turned into some great, funny memories.

School started a month later in September. We had a bad experience at the apartment complex, where a boy actually came out and threatened Cody with a BB gun. When we moved into the apartments they were brand new and we really enjoyed living there. I knew a lot of people and hated the thought of moving, but I wasn't going to stand to have another person, even a child, threaten my son with a gun. We were in the best school district in the Denver area. Jim had come over later that night after it happened. We were talking and I was crying. He also hated the thought of someone threatening Cody. I was still bound by my lease with the apartment complex. I didn't know what to do. I checked around with other apartment complexes in the area but they were more expensive than what I was paying. I couldn't afford to move. Jim knew how upset I was and wanted to offer comfort and support. But what happened next really surprised me. Without hesitation he said, "Move in with me. You guys can just move in with me. I have a house and I have room."

Jim lived out in the country on eight acres. I had never lived in the country before. His house was an hour from Denver. But I trusted him. I trusted our relationship. Jim trusted our relationship enough to ask me to move in. He wanted Cody to be able to run free on the eight acres and not have to worry about others threatening him. So I agreed and said, "If that will keep my son safe and out of harm's way, I will do it, because I would do anything for him." Jim grinned in response and the moving process started.

Up to that point, since I was raising a son alone, I didn't believe in living with a guy. Jim's house had two bedrooms and he was finishing a third one. I didn't believe in sleeping in the same room as Jim since we were not married and at that point, we were not even engaged. I didn't want to give Cody the wrong idea. Cody had his own separate room across the house from Jim's room. I was roomless, so to speak. I used part of Cody's closet and part of Jim's for my clothes. Jim said he would give up his room for me but I wouldn't let him. I slept on an air mattress outside of Cody's room. That way he knew I was close and I felt like I was doing the right thing. Jim wouldn't let me sleep out there every night. He and I took turns sleeping on the air mattress so I could have a bed. We made it work. Another great advantage was that both Jim and I were saving money, as we were splitting all of the bills. It was nice to finally have money again.

Compromise is a big part of both your personal and work relationships. You just do what you need to do to make things work and make things come together. Jim was a big blessing because he took us in. He never made a big fuss about things, and he knew that Cody and I came as a package deal.

Cody was a rough-and-tough kid. He liked to play football. He liked to wrestle. He liked to do all kinds of fun, rough-and-tough things that boys do. Much to my amazement, Jim liked that. He taught Cody how to throw a football, make a catch, tackle each other the right way and basically taught him how to play football. It was really fun to watch them out in the field or out on the acreage playing catch together and then having each other run after the ball. It's the simple things in life that amaze me. What a blessing that a wonderful man took the time out of his life to love us enough to teach Cody football. I felt truly blessed.

Have there been times in your business life when you have felt blessed? Was it because of someone else? Or a circumstance? Thank that person for the blessing you are receiving. But make sure to thank yourself for your own blessing. One thing I have found is that people forget to thank themselves. It is because you took the initiative to pursue your business that you are able to enjoy it. Keep learning, keep being creative and keep pursuing. Most importantly, keep thanking.

We moved in with Jim in October of 2000. Christmas and New Year's Eve was fast approaching. My mom flew out for Christmas and was staying with us until January 2nd. The house was small and was even smaller when we added in one more person. But it was fun to have her there and share in our first Christmas together with Jim. She didn't like the idea of us living with him, but once she realized what our sleeping arrangements were, she felt better about it. Even at age of thirty-two, she still had influence over me.

Jim and I wanted to go out on New Year's Eve, so Mom was going to stay with Cody while we went out. Admittedly, I was having adjustment issues with living in the country. I missed city living. I missed having the everyday conveniences close around me. I liked having people around me. We lived in a cul-de-sac with all of our neighbors having eight acres each. It was nice because we did have neighbors, but bad because I would have liked having people closer to me so I could have others to talk to. Jim was more solitary than I am. He loved country living. I was having a hard time getting used to it. I'm kind of spoiled. The city had everything. If I needed groceries in the middle of the night, I could go get them. Also, the night life in the city was great. I like things within reach when I need them. Country living was hard as we were thirty minutes from the nearest grocery store that wasn't open all night. Jim's house was an hour away from Denver and fifty minutes away from Colorado Springs.

Jim knew the difficulties I was having with living in the country and adapting to driving to Denver every day for work. My car's miles were racking up and I wasn't happy about it. The gravel roads were not good for my tires. Discount Tire and I got to be very good friends through my years of living in the country due to so many flat tires from the gravel road.

I wanted to go out for New Year's Eve. I wanted to go to either Denver or Colorado Springs but Jim didn't want to drive that far, especially if we were going to have a drink or two. He didn't want to be driving and I understood that. In the town of Elbert, where we lived there is a little bar called the South Forty Saloon. I had never been there and Jim said it would be fun. He figured a lot of town folk would be there to celebrate New Year's Eve. He was wrong. Maybe a handful of people were there. We first sat at the bar then decided to move to a table for more privacy. He wanted to talk since he knew I was getting upset about not going to the big city for some fun on New Year's Eve.

Don't get me wrong. I wasn't a big partier and neither was he. We hadn't seen each other drunk yet and if we did go out, we only had one or two at supper. But still, with the holiday and only one or two drinks, driving far was out of the question. I knew that, I just didn't like it. When Jim knew I was upset he always looked very concerned and would gaze at me so lovingly that it was hard to stay upset with him. He would stare me straight in the eye and ask what was wrong. How could I stay mad at that? No one had ever done that before for me and it was an awesome feeling to know someone cared. While sitting at the table, he stared at me in the eyes, so I backed down. He started to talk and said, "You know, I really adore you and Cody."

I replied, "Well, we adore you. We think it's great, and I'm still trying to adapt to living in the country. I haven't done that very well, but I'm trying."

"I realize that," he said. I appreciate so much that you are trying your best to adapt to living in the country."

"Well, it's a part of getting to know you."

Suddenly he said, "Can I ask you something?"

"Sure," I told him.

Jim right there took me by the hand, looked at me in the eye with his calm demeanor and said, "I would like to be Cody's dad. Would that be okay with you?" The look on my face must have been priceless because the look on Jim's face almost turned to terror since I wouldn't answer right away. No one had ever loved my son like I did and now I thought this man did.

After a few long moments I looked at him and said, "Yes of course, that would be great with me." But then it hit me. What was he trying to say? Did Cody's words from the past August come back to him? I even had to think a minute about where I was. I was in total shock. So I asked him, "Well, what are you trying to say? You want to marry me?"

He looked at me with his big blue eyes and a huge grin spread across his face. He said, "Yes, I want to marry you."

Talk about almost falling off my chair! I wasn't sure this was real.

Totally out of the blue it came; it was completely unexpected. I was thinking that what my son said just four months earlier was coming to fruition. I was taken aback, surprised and shocked but very excited and so happy I could hardly talk. Did he really just say he wanted to marry me and was I actually considering it? I said, "Well, if you really mean it, you would get down on one knee and actually ask me to marry you."

So he got up, got down on one knee, took my hand, and said, "Jo, will you marry me?"

I almost screamed, "Of course, I will. Hello? You just asked me to be my son's dad. Of course, I'm going to marry you. I love you to pieces, and you've just been so wonderful to us, taking us in and giving Cody and me unconditional love." I jumped up and down and the bar erupted in applause once everyone knew what had taken place. I was the happiest girl in the world. That New Year's Eve was the best I have ever had. 2001 was going to be an amazing, wonderful year.

Before we went home, Jim told me he hadn't planned on asking me that night. He wanted to wait until he had bought a ring for me, but since I wasn't having a very good time, he just decided at the last minute to ask. We got home at about one o'clock and decided to tell Cody and my mom. Upon our arrival, Mom woke up on her own to make sure it was Jim and me coming in the house. Ironically, Cody woke up shortly thereafter. He must have known. We told them both at the same time. Cody started screaming in excitement and jumping up and down. He ran to me and hugged me, then ran to Jim. The first thing Cody did was check my finger for a ring. I told him it was unexpected, so Jim didn't have time to buy me a ring. The disappointment was obvious on his face, but he was excited we were engaged. My mom was very happy for us too. I didn't get much sleep that night because of all of the excitement and the fun planning we had to do. The joy of the night kept running through my mind. I knew his parents would be really excited too. I couldn't wait to tell them. I'd been a single mom for almost ten years. I was so happy and so excited that I was going to be Jim's wife.

We didn't know when we wanted to get married. We talked about maybe a year or two. Neither one of us was in any big rush. This was my second marriage and Jim's first. We had adjusted to our living arrangements and were content living as a family unit that way.

Jim's mom and dad were wintering down in Texas that New Year's. I was so excited to tell them that we called the next morning. Evelyn answered. Once Jim told her the news, I could hear her in the background on the phone, very excited. She asked when we were getting married and Jim told her not for a year or two. She replied "No, no, no, you guys need to get married right away. You need to get married right away. You need to get married before I pass away." She wasn't sick. As far as we knew, she was going to live a long time.

Jim said, "Mom, you aren't sick and we are in no big rush." They talked for about thirty minutes. After he hung up, I could tell she had pressured him into getting married this year.

After he hung up the phone, I asked him what she said.

He said, "She wants us married right away but I still think we should wait. What do you think?"

After sleeping on it, I had a change of heart. Deep down inside, since we were now engaged, I would feel more complete as a family, especially for Cody. So I was in agreement with his mom to get married that year. After careful thought and consideration, he agreed. We set September 29, 2001 as our wedding day.

This was on New Year's Day, and that night we were going out for supper with friends. Because of Jim's unexpected proposal the night before, there was no ring. Unexpected events can be bad or good. Sometimes out-of-the-blue decisions just have to be made and you take the consequences along with it. I was not upset I didn't have a ring but Cody was. He asked Jim repeatedly when he was going to buy me a ring. Jim didn't have an answer to that. Cody was relentless. "When are you going to buy my mom a ring?" Again Jim didn't know. We were both trying to save money and that was an unexpected expense. A good expense but unexpected.

On our way to supper, Cody wanted to stop by a big department store to check out rings. He was obsessed with me having one. Grandma had given Cody $20 for some chores he had done around the house. Cody had that money with him that night. We were looking at rings and saw that they were all expensive and out of our price range. I told Cody we would shop another time for rings. That didn't stop him. He wanted me to have something special for the engagement. It was the sweetest thing ever to see him so vigilant about me having something for our engagement.

He wandered over to the earrings and said, "Mom come over here." The earrings he was looking at were between $20 and $100. They were hanging on a stand where he could look at and feel them. He wanted me to look too, so I did. We looked at several pairs before he found the ones he liked and so did I. He said, "Mom, would you like these ones?"

I told him, "Yes, they are very beautiful."

They were $21.50. He didn't have enough money. He looked sad and bewildered. With his gutsy personality, he went to Jim and said, "Can I borrow five bucks to buy my mom these earrings for your engagement?"

Jim agreed. He pulled out five dollars from his jean pockets and Cody paid for the earrings. After he paid for them, he said, "Mom, put them on so everyone can see that you have pretty jewelry for your engagement."

It was so precious; I had tears in my eyes. I was so proud of Cody. The earrings were beautiful and I called them "my lucky earrings." I put them on with joy and had never felt so much endearment than at that moment.

What if we took that much endearment into our businesses? Cody was determined to get me those earrings or some type of jewelry. When in business, we need to make arrangements in our hearts and minds about what we want and what we want it to look like. If you are trying for the diamond but end up with something less, it's okay. It just means you have to work harder for what you want. I was content with the earrings because I knew someday I would get the ring.

Planning a second marriage is definitely different and easier than planning a first one. There were many doubts, but also a great deal of enthusiasm. There came some times when I thought, *I don't want to do this as big as I did the first wedding, but yet Jim has never been married, so I want him to have a nice wedding.* Jim didn't want anything big or fancy and neither did I.

Cody didn't stop on his rant for me to have a ring either. I finally got one two months after our engagement. I felt sorry for poor Jim during those two months. Cody was happily surprised when we came home and I had a ring on.

The excitement of the months of planning never ceased. It helped to be older and more mature planning this wedding. I had two bridesmaids and my maid of honor. Jim had two groomsmen and his dad as best man. Those were easy to pick out. We had Jim's dad's best friend marry us in the church his dad attended. Sometimes when fear and doubt entered my mind I relied on my friends to help. Jim and my friends were always there to help pick me up. That is what we need in life: to have someone to turn to when fears and doubts enter our minds. I would think thoughts like, *What happens if this marriage ends in divorce? What happens if Jim doesn't love us to the end of time?*

The "what-ifs" can wear you down. If you succumb to those, you might lose out on the best thing that can happen to you. We need to let others know our fears and doubts so they can help us realize that everything will turn out the way it is supposed to. Jim was a big help in the planning area too. He would listen with an open mind and give me his opinions. We worked as a team.

If you're in business with somebody else or you are thinking about it, you really need to listen to what their ideas are and what they have to say. Then you can work together as a team to bring that to fruition, change it or delete it. That has really helped me. Working with Jim through the wedding helped me in my business to work with other people. I finally had someone who was willing to help me, which in turned helped me in my business. I could relate to others and listen to their concerns and ideas with an open mind.

Our wedding day was set for September 29, 2001. Unfortunate history was made on September 11, 2001, now known as 9/11. Flights were canceled and our world was in shock and horror. I had a few people flying in for the wedding. What would happen if there was still no flying at that time? That was how my mother was going to get to come. Fear and doubt eventually turned to ease and excitement again. As luck would have it, by the time our wedding came, the flights had been resumed.

It was a gorgeous Colorado day. The sky was as blue as blue could be. The sun was shining brightly and the temperature was in the high 70s. It was perfect. Cody wore a black tux like the rest of the groomsmen did. It was cute, as his tux shirt was too big for him. The guys took him in the backroom and duct taped the back of his shirt together so it wouldn't hang out from under his coat. Sometimes we have to make adjustments in life to our different circumstances and our wedding day was no different. Duct tape works for anything they said, and I believed them.

The night before the wedding, Cody had spent the night with my mom in a hotel room. During the night he had fallen off the bed and hit the side of his eye on the nightstand. He had a big black-and-blue spot on the side of his eye. My mom was upset and thought I would be too. Cody was three weeks' shy of being ten years old. That is what kids his age did. I wasn't upset and laughed it off. What fun is life if we can't laugh at things that happen to us? Just make adjustments and move on.

Cody was the one I chose to walk me down the aisle. Since my dad had passed away when I was eleven, the next best thing was my son. As we waited at the entrance of the sanctuary, I looked down at him and said, "Are you as excited as I am?" He nodded his head up and down nervously. Just before the processional music started he took my arm in his and I looked at him once again. I said, "Are you ready to go, buddy?"

He replied, "I am, Mom."

I said, "All right, bud. Let's do this."

"Okay," he declared.

As we were walking down the aisle, his smile was so radiant and bright and he had the cutest nervous nine-year-old laugh that was precious to everyone. He was so proud and so handsome in his tuxedo. I was so proud that he was walking me down the aisle. When Jack, the minister, asked who was to give this woman to Jim, Cody responded, "I do!" He then gave my arm to Jim and took his place standing between Jim and his dad while the ceremony proceeded.

After the minister pronounced us husband and wife, we kissed short and softly. But Cody chimed in and was kind of yelling, "Kiss her. Kiss her. Kiss her, Jim. Kiss her." So we kissed again and Cody tilted his head and just stared and smiled at us in amazement. Jim and I turned around to face the congregation and Jack announced us as a family. "I now pronounce you, Jim, Donna Jo, and Cody as a family." People started clapping, and we walked down the aisle. It was the greatest feeling in the world that we were all family now under the oath of God.

It was just the most beautiful, peaceful day of my life. It was a blessing to have most of our friends and family there to share in our special day. It was so serene and I just knew there was no better peace in my life at that point than having us be family. The marriage was meant to be. It was a beautiful union of two people and my son, and I couldn't have asked for anything better.

A week after our wedding, we headed back to South Dakota for a reception there. I had quite a few family members who lived in Minnesota and South Dakota who were not able to make it to Colorado for the wedding. It was fun to see all of them. Jim was good about verbalizing what he liked or didn't like about something. He was really happy to have that reception back in South Dakota. He was welcomed with open arms, and he felt loved, just as much or even more than how he felt in Colorado. I always loved when we would come home to South Dakota for a visit because of that warmth and the way we felt loved.

Delayed gratification seems to be a thing of the past these days. It is hard to wait and be patient. Being in a hurry can kill creativity and compassion. To be patient, you must learn to be good to yourself. You are your Number One supporter or detractor. God didn't put us on this earth to hurt ourselves. There had been a couple of times I could have caved in and married other guys before I met Jim. They were wonderful men and brought a lot of fun and newness to my life. But I knew what I wanted in a man and it was worth the wait.

Timing is everything. There were times during my single years when I never thought I would find the love of my life. I tried for years to find a wonderful, loving man who would love my son and me unconditionally. It was frustrating and sometimes depressing. Since Denver was so big, I didn't think it would take long to find a man. I was wrong. When I wanted a man so desperately, either none or the wrong ones appeared. But when I wasn't looking, out of the blue he came into my life.

Things like that can happen with business, as well. You can reach and search for that perfect client but don't find them. Then there will be times when you're not even looking for what you want or need, and it comes into your life, and you have to embrace that. You have to take what you can get on a daily basis and believe there's going to be better coming. Just remember, timing and patience are critical and success comes when you work hard at what you want. When you work hard, you place yourself where good luck can find you.

There have been times when it's been difficult for me to overcome fear. I was afraid of a second marriage. I was afraid of starting a new business. What I realized was the fear that overcame me was exactly the fear I should pursue.

Fear only holds you back. It makes you think negatively about your life and the ability to move forward. In business, personal relationships, or life in general, sometimes it's easy to be taken aback by fear and never take that step forward. In reality, the opposite should be the reaction. Take that step forward and get to the next level. Do whatever you have to do to overcome that fear. Once you conquer it, you are going to feel like you can conquer anything. What a wonderful freeing feeling.

There are women who are scared of the financial and emotional insecurity of being alone or having to figure things out on their own. You can make it on your own just fine. I did it. I did it for many years. If you don't have a spouse or partner, confide in someone who will help you get to the financial security that you desire. For emotional security, lean on others for support. A lot of my friends don't own businesses, but they are always supportive and never condemn. If they did, they wouldn't be my friends. It is also imperative to either get a business coach or a business owner who can be a mentor for you.

When I married Jim, I found the right partner for financial and emotional security. He was great at saving money. I did save a little before I met him but I learned a lot from him and respected his viewpoints. It wasn't always fun, as I would rather spend then save; but in the long run I knew it was for the best. We got into many disagreements over spending money. I wanted it my way and he wanted it his. We had to come to an agreement, which we almost always did. Knowing I had somebody I could work together with on our business and personal finances really did help. Utilize friends and partners/spouses to help you with the security that you need. Feeling like you have someone in your corner to help support and guide you makes you accountable.

Choose to imagine what's possible, instead of giving way to the fear of impossibility. Choose to visualize the vast potential of any given idea, instead of anticipating the barriers and challenges that might stand in your way. Choose to let go of every preconceived notion, every "voice of reason" and every cause and effect. Choose to dream Big, think Big, play Big, feel Big and BE Big. Eliminate all of the feelings of smallness and lack. Choose to refuse to fall victim to circumstance; and instead, create your own reality. Choose to ignite a spark within you that burns so brightly it can never be darkened again. You hold the power to make it happen. Choose to Believe.

– Tara Holling

CHAPTER 6

The Early Years and Our Move to South Dakota

WHEN I met Jim he had a butterfly tattoo on his chest. He loved that tattoo. His favorite saying was from Muhammad Ali: "Float like a butterfly and sting like a bee." That's why he got the tattoo. He loved to make the wings move up and down when he flexed his chest muscles. Cody used to chuckle when he did that. At first, Jim was embarrassed to show me the tattoo. We were in a pool at a recreation center when I first saw it. He was slow to take off his shirt. Cody encouraged him to get in the water. So, slowly, he took off his shirt and jumped in the water before I could see it. I said, "Hey, you are hiding something from me." And he came out of the water and showed me.

At first I didn't think anything about it. I don't like tattoos but since it was done, I couldn't do much about it. He explained he had developed Hepatitis C from getting the tattoo. He was embarrassed to show it to me after he told me. His Hepatitis C was diagnosed two years before I met him. He had gone through Interferon shots and when we met, he was in remission and doing great. I would have never known he had been sick. He explained that the Interferon shots had made him very sick and he missed a lot of work due to throwing up, severe fatigue and the other side effects from it. Once the doctors cleared him and stated that he was in remission, he went back to normal activities. He was doing so great when we met that he was working normal hours and playing softball. Once our relationship got more serious I did start to notice little things with him, like that he got tired easily and some days didn't feel good, but he kept going. Jim wasn't a big complainer. If he didn't feel good, he became quiet and retreated to the bedroom.

After we were married, I started looking for other opportunities for work. I was tired of driving to Denver every day and it was taking a toll on my car and my attitude. I was ready to start looking at work-from-home opportunities.

I first got the bug to work from home full-time when I was single and still living in Denver. While working my state job, I was part of a pilot project to work from home and only come into the office one day a week. I fell in love with it. I was loving being able to take Cody to school and pick him up. I did that for three months until the pilot project ended. Once it had ended, I wanted more. I informed Jim what a great experience it was for me and he knew I wanted to be able to spend more time and do more things with Cody. Being married now made that dream a little easier.

I had heard about network marketing companies and wanted to learn more but wanted his approval first. When I approached him about starting a network marketing company he said, "I'm going to let you do that, because you're better at talking to people and networking with people than I am. But then when you get that going, maybe we can both work from home." I was disappointed that he didn't want to work the opportunity with me though. I was hoping he would come in with me full-time. But first I needed to find something that would fit our needs and our schedule.

I scoured the web, the newspapers and listened for ads on the radio about work-from-home jobs. Since we lived in the country between Denver and Colorado Springs, I looked and listened in both places. By this time Cody was involved in sports and active in school activities so I wanted to be able to participate in all of those with him.

While researching the work-from-home opportunities I knew not to fall for the ones where I had to pay something to get something. Those are never worthy of your time or money. Those types of businesses are almost always a scam. But I did find one that caught my eye. It was a network marketing company where I could work from home plus go to Colorado Springs for meetings. I liked that because I still wanted to be in contact with people and knew I would need the support to learn the business. So I contacted them and got signed up. I went to a lot of their seminars, a lot of their classes and after six months I was the third-best seller for the month of March that the company had.

Thoughts were running through my mind that this was pretty good and we could make this work. Jim and I would lie in bed at night, staring out at the stars, talking about how someday we would make all of this money and be able to retire early. It was great dreaming like that. Jim would tell me how proud he was of me and I felt it.

I learned a lot from working with this company and the biggest thing I learned was to be a leader. I had always wanted to be a leader at work. This job gave me that opportunity. I went out on my own and signed people up under me. I studied and got my life insurance license, which was a big accomplishment. This company opened up doors for me that I didn't think existed. I had the biggest confidence boost after passing the life insurance exam. I hadn't had any classes since college where I had to take a test. I was proud of myself.

Unfortunately, after about nine months, that business faded for me. I wasn't getting the business that I wanted anymore, and I was still driving to Denver for my full-time job. After getting home, then I would drive to Colorado Springs for business meetings and meeting with potential customers. I was spending less time with my family instead of more time. Cody would get upset when I would have to leave at night so I decided to look for something else.

A few months later, Jim called me excitedly, saying I needed to meet with this man he just talked to about another network marketing opportunity. Jim had known him for a while but never knew what he did until that day. It was a Saturday in Greenwood Village, Colorado at a city sponsored fishing derby where Jim was working. Ferris came up and was speaking with Jim about the fishing derby when he asked if Jim was satisfied with his life and income. Jim said yes to his life, but no to the income. He wanted us to be making more and for me to be able to stay home with Cody. He told Ferris about my previous network marketing gig and that I wanted to work from home for Cody. So Jim and I set up a time to talk to Ferris and his family the next day. We went to the meeting and were so excited about the opportunity that we signed up and started working our new business.

We chose to start off slowly and build ourselves up to it. That company was kind of a lifesaver for us, because it was selling nutritional products. All three of us started on them and Jim's health started to improve. He wasn't as sick as often and he had more energy. My health and Cody's were already good, but we saw improvements too. My allergies got better and Cody's overall health improved. This time the meetings were in Denver and that helped since I could go over my lunch hour or right after work. During the progression of this business, we built up a big team. While we were building the business, Jim and I discussed my going part-time at my job so I could spend more time with the new business.

While still working my job, I built a nice team at work. I would bring in pizza and pop for lunch and then talk with others about the products. They got free food and I got to do my presentations. We also held meetings at hotel rooms at night and on the weekends. Jim got involved with this business. He was great at talking to people then giving me their contact information. I was the closer. He liked that and he had goals of how many people to talk to each day. If he hadn't met his goal, he would stop on his way home from work just so he could talk to people. We made a great team. We had been debating if I was going to quit my job altogether and go full-time with the business since it was going so well. I had worked my job and the business part-time for almost a year when we were thinking about this.

If you have a partner in your business, do each of you have a different expertise that you focus on? It is great when you can play off each other. One gets clients and the other one closes them. Work out a system so this can happen. Are you solo? There are no problems with you playing all of the roles. Just know what you are good at and what you need to learn more about. Education is key.

Just about the time all of that was happening, my mother was having some vision issues back in South Dakota. She had come out to see us and told us she had to have eye surgery and there was a good possibility she might lose vision in her eye. My mother had never remarried after my dad passed away, so she was alone. I had a brother who lived there, but really he wasn't any help in these kinds of situations. At the time my other brother and his family lived in Utah and we lived in Colorado. I said to her, "Why don't you move out here to Colorado so we can take care of you?" But she didn't want to do that. She was still working at the time and trying to get to retirement.

The one thing I always wanted to do with my life was please my mom. I think it stems from when my dad passed away and I would see her cry. I hated that. I want people to be happy and not sad. So I would take it upon myself to make things better if I could. I knew moving away from South Dakota was disappointing to her, but raising my son the way I was also gave her great joy. As a mom, she saw how happy Cody and I were, so in turn she was happy. As a mom myself, I always feel better when my son is happy. I was disappointed she wouldn't move to Colorado but she had lived all of her adult life in South Dakota. She wasn't great at change.

I wasn't sure how she would do if she moved out of state. I still considered her young as she was in her mid-sixties, but she felt she was getting older and didn't want to move either. She was scared of the surgery. I told her I would come back and help out afterward. When I was home taking care of her, I really started thinking more seriously about moving back to South Dakota. Through the years of traveling back there, I would see the Welcome to South Dakota sign and I always felt a big relief. My shoulders would fall and I would whisper, "I am home." It was a peaceful, relaxing feeling.

Cody was getting older and would soon be in middle school. I liked the elementary school he was in, but then he would need to transition to a big, new middle and high school. That made me nervous. I had respect for the school system but also felt uneasy with it being so large compared to what I grew up in. The high school he would have gone to in Colorado had over 4,000 kids. My graduating class was 132 and his sixth-grade class alone was over twice that. The more I thought about it, the more I was talking myself into moving back to South Dakota. I knew it would take Jim a while to warm up to the idea. Once I returned from taking care of my mom I started dropping hints about moving.

He gave me a stunned look. "Why would we?"

I explained how I felt about the school system and how Mom might need help as she got older. Jim was a native of Colorado and loved his home state. The one thing he didn't like was the traffic of all of the outsiders coming in. He complained about that a lot. His family had all moved out of Colorado so we were the only ones left. Moving to South Dakota would be better for Cody, I felt, since the schools are smaller and we would live in the same town where he went to school. I knew the town and school district where I wanted to move and it would be close to my mom. That way we could go to all of his sporting and school events and still build this network marketing company. Plus, I still had quite a few family members living in South Dakota and the sense of security that gave me was greater than the desire to live in Colorado.

It took me a full year to really convince him that moving back to South Dakota was the way to go. Our network marketing company was doing very well. He was still working full-time, I was still working part-time and using the network marketing business as the other half of our money for full-time living. We went back a couple of times to South Dakota to look at houses. Jim's only requirement for a house was that we have no backyard neighbors. We found one we both liked, and there were no back neighbors. It was a split foyer home; when you walked in you could either walk upstairs or downstairs. As we entered, I walked upstairs as he walked downstairs. I looked down on him and said, "I absolutely love this house."

In his sweet tone and calm demeanor, he looked up at me and said, "Then you will have this house." My heart melted. I had never owned my own house before. When it was just Cody and me, we always lived in apartments. Then we moved into

Jim's house. So there had never been any that I had picked out or owned. There is nothing more special than picking out a house together that you know will become your family's home.

In August 2004, we got the papers signed on the new house in South Dakota, we got somebody to rent our house in Colorado, and we moved to South Dakota. Cody was going into the seventh grade. For me, it couldn't have been better timing.

Cody seemed excited about the move except when it came to leaving his friends in Colorado. The night before we moved, Cody was lying on an air mattress, since all the beds were loaded on the truck. He looked at me with sad eyes and said, "Mom, I hate you for making me leave Colorado and my friends."

And I said, "Cody, I love you and I know South Dakota will be a much better place for you."

We weren't even living in South Dakota a week and he was loving it. He said "Mom, I love it here, I love it here."

And I replied, "I knew you would. It just takes time to make friends but you made them quickly." Within two weeks of moving, he started school and our new lives began.

That year of trying to convince Jim to move was one of anxiety and patience. I often find that to be true of running a business, too. Moving in the right direction is a long, hard step, but knowing it is the right move makes it worthwhile. Throughout that year, since he was being stubborn about moving, I tried different tactics and learned how and when to approach him. Coming on too strong was not working but being too subtle wasn't working either. Being with someone for a while, if you pay attention, you will learn their different times and attitudes and when to approach them. It worked as long as I put my faith in my system.

Before we moved back to South Dakota, it was starting to become more noticeable that Jim didn't feel well, although we were taking the nutritional products. He was missing more work and was getting tired. I remember thinking if we could just get moved to South Dakota, everything would turn out alright. What was I thinking? Why would a move make everything turn out okay? Maybe I was running away from the problem that caused it. Moving was exciting and something new and fresh to look forward to. God wouldn't give us more medical issues when we moved, would he? Being close to family would help settle all of our woes. It would give us comfort and help if we needed it. These were things that I was thinking.

My mind was creating a barrier to the truth that I didn't want to believe and take on. Once we got settled into our home and got Cody off to school, we both started looking for jobs. Jim's health was holding up. I would ask him every day for a year how he felt and most of the time he would say, "Good." So in my mind the move was justified, and he was looking good too: strong, muscular and healthy.

Moving back to South Dakota was wonderful because I felt like I was home. Jim liked it because the town was small, Cody was prospering and Mom had moved to the same town we lived in. What I didn't count on was that Mom would give up driving. I tried to encourage her to keep driving, just only during the day, but she wouldn't hear of it. She was too afraid of hitting someone; especially a child. I admire her for that. With the vision gone in one eye and the other eye not good, she turned in her license. It's hard to see parents getting older and giving up their independence. I now had to be her taxi driver. I still wanted her to be the busy mom driving all over town like she used to. But her reality was that she couldn't, and I had to face my new reality which was being part of the sandwich generation: taking care of parents while raising your own family. As much as I hated it, that was my new reality.

We need to face our realities and deal with them. How you handle them shows a lot about the type of person you are. My realities were mine and I chose to deal with them. I didn't like them. There were days when I felt sorry for myself. I tried hard not to complain. I just wanted to be a mom, daughter and wife without adversity. Those were enough responsibilities. But God intervened when I started feeling this way. I could hear in the back of my mind that is why I was put on this earth: to care for others. To live and love generously and not complain. Go forth with grace and put forth your best effort toward caring for others. But never forget to care for yourself.

We need to face our business realities and deal with them. You wanted your business; now it is time to take care of it. Are there difficulties you are not addressing? Who are you taking care of in your business who might need a nudge to do it without your help? Sometimes all that's needed is your encouragement to get it done.

After my mom had been retired for a couple of years, I urged her to start using our local bus in town to go to the grocery store, local doctor's appointments and church. Plus, it freed up my time by not having to drive her as much. Once she found she could do it, she felt more confident and loves taking the bus now. To watch her was like giving a child a new bike. Once her confidence built up, her world opened up again. It gives her more independence and the ability to be with other people.

Having that confidence, just knowing you made the right decision, helps you feel empowered. It is hard to be confident when your mind is cluttered. Struggling with what decision to make is mind-cluttering and frustrating. It can be stressful. If something becomes too stressful for me, I tend to focus my attention elsewhere. I have learned, and unfortunately am still learning the hard way, just to make a decision and not procrastinate. Most often it just takes one step of courage and strength to make a decision.

Confidence also comes from having commitment, which relates to responsibility. Without commitment we are not gaining. We all have some type of responsibility in our lives. Are you taking yours seriously? What decision are you putting off that needs to be made now? When you're in business, responsibility can be all yours. You may not always make the right decisions and it can be a tough scenario, but making a decision and sticking with it gives you both credibility and confidence that will promote future growth. Confidence can come from winning and losing.

Have I not commanded you? Be strong and courageous. Do not be frightened, and do not be dismayed, for the Lord your God is with you wherever you go. (Joshua 1:9)

Learning new skills and pursuing new opportunities helps you grow. Do you want more income while building your business? Maybe look into something, including another business that can bring in extra income. Also, make sure that business or income-producing job is gaining you networking and communication skills. These are needed in your own business. The more contacts you can meet the more people you can network your business to. It's a win-win situation. You are making more money and you are making connections.

Learning social and communication skills is always great no matter what you do. Is yours a job where all you do is sit at your desk and you never see other people? Join different groups around town. Going to meetings for the network marketing companies I worked with really helped me get out and meet a lot more people. It expanded my social group and I could learn a lot of business skills through these companies. That has expanded over to my work-from-home business. The more skills you can acquire and feel comfortable with, the more you can expand your business. The more confident you become, the more people will be attracted to you. Driving my mom and one of her friends around has given me the thought for years to open up a taxi service, because I am confident now with picking up people and taking them places.

Always be learning new skills and taking opportunities to meet new people. Some days are easier than others. Do you ever just feel like sitting in front of your computer and never leaving? Those are the days you should be out in public and meeting new people. God put you there for a reason. He doesn't want you to stop. He is always giving fresh new days in which to learn new things; breathe in fresh new air and love the business that you are doing.

CHAPTER 7
Starting My Own Business

Long before I went into business for myself, I knew I no longer wanted to sit in an office, all day, staring at walls and a computer screen. It didn't matter if I was working for the government or the private sector; it seemed like offices were all the same. Yes, some were much better than others and I always came away with something useful from the job. The one thing I did love about working in an office was the people. And yet, one of the things I really disliked was the people; or rather the gossip from the people.

I found myself succumbing to the gossip ring and I didn't like it. Someone would act like your friend just to hear gossip. It was my own fault for falling into it, but it happened a lot. As I grew older I really started to resent it. One time while working a job I didn't like, I decided to start a little rumor about myself and see if I recognized it when it came back to me. By the time it got back to me, it had exploded into something completely different from what I had originally said. Does that sound mean? Possibly. But I did it to make a point to myself. If the people I worked with didn't care enough to come straight out and talk to me about the rumor, why would I want to be friends with them? It was a turning point for me. It fueled me to find a better work opportunity and the start of my quest to work from home.

At each job I had to be at work by eight, work a couple of hours, get a break, work, get lunch, work again, get another break and then eventually go home. In between there were meetings I had to attend and the phones rang a lot. I hated having someone else tell me what time I needed to come to in and when I needed to take a break. There were days when I would sit at my desk and dream of working from home, setting my own hours and doing what I wanted. For me it was much better than working for someone else. I knew I wanted my freedom.

While working for corporate America, I would attend the meetings that I was required to. There were days I felt I knew more than the presenter at the meeting. I would speak my ideas and say what I felt was needed. There were many times I was heard and the ideas were noted. It made me feel good when that would happen. But more often than not, they weren't heard and were overlooked. That was very frustrating. Then, even worse was when the idea I vocalized and got shot down was turned into an idea or realization by someone else. Ever have that happen? You present a great idea and it is turned down, but someone else brings it up and gets credit? Doesn't make sense, does it?

When I worked in Iowa, my supervisor didn't like women on his team. He wanted an all-male staff. I am pretty easy to get along with and I can take a lot. I had been working under him about a year and a half when he decided to time me on how long I took in the bathroom.

One time after I came back, he came over to my office and said, "Do you know how long you were in the bathroom?"

I gave him a bewildered look and said, "No. Why?"

"You were in that bathroom seven minutes and forty-nine seconds."

My eyes lit up and my mouth dropped; I couldn't believe what he had just said. For a moment I paused in total disbelief but then responded with, "Well, guess what? I could have been in there ten minutes and forty-nine seconds, but I decided to come out early."

He then proceeded to tell me I needed to limit how long I was in the bathroom. I decided to blow the whistle on him. I was in my late twenties at that time and didn't feel like putting up with his tactics anymore. I was actually proud of myself for turning him in. I try to get along with everybody and not make waves. At that time in my life, I normally wouldn't have said anything to anybody but turning him in made me feel proud. Others thanked me as well since I was not the only one he had harassed. I reported him to our administrator and he took disciplinary action against him. After that, the supervisor was very nice to me and we got along for the rest of my tenure there.

When I worked for another state government office, we had a top-notch official who worked directly under the President of the United States come to visit with us. I was on the liaison panel to talk with him. We were implementing a new process at our facility which was actually kind of scary. It dealt with how we explained being turned down for benefits to the public. I knew this was not a good idea. I vocalized it to my boss and the others in our office. I explained if we were going to do this, we needed protection, like having an armed officer. At that time, we didn't have security cameras, locked doors or even a front office receptionist. Anyone could have walked through the door. How scary for all of us working there. Before they implemented the new procedure, they did get a secured door and front receptionist. After the implementation, we were evacuated several times due to bomb threats and suicidal clients. We were all very frustrated and fearful. Thankfully the procedure was halted and we went back to the way we normally did things.

These two scenarios were some of the things I encountered in my work life. We all have them, don't we? Can you name one or two things that have happened to you? Instead of dwelling on them, make that incident propel you to something better and greater. This scary incident was what prompted me to decide I needed to make a change and make sure Cody and I were safe. I hadn't met Jim yet so I started to think of who would take care of my son if I weren't around. Cody's dad is a decent man but I didn't want him raising Cody. I wanted to raise Cody and do right by him. My mind was flushed with these thoughts for quite some time after those scary incidents. That was probably the first time I really started to question where my life was headed and what my purpose was on earth was. Was I supposed to work for someone else the rest of my life? But how would I start something on my own? And what?

After meeting Jim and starting the network marketing businesses, I knew working from home was the best scenario for my family and me. These businesses were great because I met a lot of people. You never know when your past will catch up with your present. While building my business, I attended a lot of networking events. I was in the business of meeting new people and attending these events really helped with that goal. I handed out a lot of business cards and in return got many back. While attending an eWomenNetwork event in Colorado, I met a woman who was putting together a seminar for women called Women's Web Workshop. The year was 2004 and it was about helping women learn how to have an online business. She did a drawing for free attendance worth $250. And I won!

I was so excited and knew I had to attend. The problem was the event was happening after our move to South Dakota. That didn't stop me. Jim knew how excited I was about the opportunity and was more excited when he found out I got to go for free. I drove back to Denver for the weekend of the seminar. That weekend changed my life. I was more excited than I had been in a long time. I met great people and business coaches who could help me propel into the future. Learning how to start an online business seemed just the avenue I wanted to take. I was good on the computer, liked searching the web and was good at typing. I had administrative skills and had great customer service skills. I knew those traits would be needed when I considered a work-from-home job.

At that seminar, I learned a lot about virtual systems. It opened up a whole new world to me. There were so many things online I could do. A couple of ideas she threw out were selling on eBay and Craigslist. Going out and buying items at a discounted rate then selling them or selling what you have in your home. This way you are making extra revenue that could possibly turn into a full-time job. I also learned about virtual personal assistants and other types of businesses women can start on the web. When the seminar was over and as I drove back to South Dakota, I was so excited and energized. I had fire in my belly and knew there was something out there that I could do. That was probably the fastest driving trip I had ever made from Colorado to South Dakota. I still have the completion certificate hanging on my wall by my desk from this conference.

After coming home from that conference, I interviewed and was named Managing Director of South Dakota for eWomenNetwork. I put my network marketing business aside to work this business. It was a monthly networking event for women business owners. This was my first experience starting a business at home. I brought in speakers and attended several networking events around the area to help spread the word. I developed a database of a thousand names in less than three months. I loved it since I was able to network with a lot of men and women in business. eWomenNetwork gave me the opportunity to explore my networking skills and bring people together who would have never met without it. That gave me a thrill to know I was helping other business owners connect.

eWomenNetwork has a yearly conference in Texas. As Managing Director, I was required to attend. I enjoyed going to conferences and learning new ideas. Through my work as a Managing Director, I had learned about virtual assistants and thought about hiring one myself to keep me current on my workload. However, I was afraid of the cost. Jim was tight with money and I felt guilty about spending it, knowing I wasn't making a lot of money at the time. We discussed it and agreed I had to do it all myself in order to succeed. Looking back, this was not a good decision but it led me to where I was supposed to be.

At the conference I had bought a book by one of the speakers I had heard. It is called The Accidental Millionaire by Stefanie Frank. While on the plane flying to Minneapolis, Minnesota, I was sitting in the middle seat reading the book. Suddenly, a lady from across the aisle in the middle seat leaned over and said, "Hey, do you know the author of that book?"

I looked at her and then pointed to myself, asking, "Are you talking to me?"

"Yes," she said. "Do you know Stefanie?"

I said, "No, but I listened to her at the conference and liked what she had to say, so I wanted to buy her book."

"Well, I am her virtual assistant," she announced.

My eyes lit up and I could hardly contain myself. I wanted to talk to her. Something sparked in me and I knew then I wanted to be a virtual assistant. She introduced herself as Jean and we started a conversation. When the other people around us started to get annoyed, we decided to chat for a few minutes once we landed.

After landing, I had to catch another plane to South Dakota; I only had a few minutes. I learned that Jean lived in Minneapolis and had been a virtual assistant for several years. We exchanged business cards and I asked if I could contact her sometime. She was very open and said sure. I had no idea then how much my life changed on the airplane that day.

I had been a Managing Director for about a year and loved it, but unfortunately the numbers were dwindling. I had been working with a business coach trying to figure out a way to keep it going. The different ideas we tried were not working. eWomenNetwork is an awesome organization and I loved being part of it. Unfortunately, the cost was prohibitive and I eventually had to determine when I would let it go. I wrestled with that since I loved what I was doing and the networking that came with it. I thrive at networking but couldn't keep going with my paycheck dwindling along with the attendance.

Returning from the conference, I had a call with my business coach. I was so excited that the first thing I told her was, "I met this gal who is a virtual assistant."

My business coached stopped me right there and said, "That's it; that is what you are supposed to do. You are supposed to be a virtual assistant." I knew it too.

While putting together ideas for my new virtual assistant business, I decided to contact Jean to see if she had any extra work for me to do. This way I could get some experience and be more employable to others. Jean was so gracious and so nice. I asked her for tips and pointers and she generously mentored me. She told me she made appointments; she helped clients do website design and developed databases. She produced online newsletters. She did customer service, email support for clients and made travel reservations. She performed a wide variety of tasks depending on what each client's needs were. I was amazed. This was exactly what I wanted to do. Then I got the guts to ask her if she had any extra work she could filter to me. She said, "Well, I'm okay with my work, but my husband just started an online business with a membership website and we need some help with that." I could barely contain myself. I was so excited, knowing I was going to be working with them.

By this time, I had quit eWomenNetwork and found another full-time job. I told her I needed the income from that job. She understood and was okay with me working the business part-time at night. Some weeks there would be more work than others. We set up another time to talk after that as she wanted to consult with her husband regarding what tasks I should do. When I am excited on the phone I am so glad the other person can't see me. I was doing a happy dance all around my desk and throwing my arms up in the air. I got my first client as a virtual assistant and it was all due to being in the right place at the right time with the right intention and vision in my mind.

What a true blessing, as I knew this would all come together. Isn't this true when you have the right intention and vision for a business and then it comes true? It is not luck. It is putting your intention out there so it can come to you. What are *your* intentions?

After that, they not only became my clients but also my friends. If it hadn't been for Jean and her generous mentoring, I don't think I'd be where I am today. I give her almost all my credit because when I first started my virtual assistant work, I had dial-up internet. I had no fax machine or scanner. I had a printer that kind of worked and only had a cell phone; no work phone. We didn't have a lot of money for the extras so I made do with what we had.

You don't need a lot of money to start a business. You don't need all of the fancy equipment and the best of everything. Start where you are and work it from there. The other things will come in time. I started with barely anything and couldn't afford a lot. You can always work your way up as you get more experience.

Jean took me by the hand and showed me how to do things. A lot of the things she said she did for clients were things I didn't know how to do. That scared me. She spent hours with me training me how to do specific tasks for their business. Sometimes we would both get frustrated but she never gave up on me. If I didn't get it, I would Google it. This was before YouTube. I would spend hours researching certain tasks and learning on my own.

Cody was in eighth grade at that time. My friends would call and ask me to go out and do things with them. I had to turn them down a lot. I gave up spending time with my friends so that I could work the business. I never missed out on Cody's activities, but I knew this business was more important than my social life. I wanted to impress Jean because I knew she could take me places and teach me. The work she gave me came first and my social life came second. It was awkward since my friends didn't understand what I was doing, but I didn't care. I was on a mission to make it work. She started me off at $13 an hour and it was the best money I had ever made.

After about three months of working with Jean and Steve, Jean encouraged me to get high speed internet. She said, "If you want to progress with this business you need to get high speed internet. Don't do this dial-up anymore." I fretted about that because again, we didn't have a lot of money. There will be struggles with starting your own business without a lot of money; you just have to gradually build into things and that's exactly what I did.

One avenue I used to spread the word about my business was attending network events several hours a week. I knew networking was successful as I had done it for both the eWomenNetwork and network marketing companies I started. This included joining my local Chamber of Commerce. I actually joined two of them: the one in my town and the one in the adjoining town, which is a lot bigger. I would also go to BNI (Business Networking International). These places all had costs to belong. I was trying to keep my costs low so I also attended local groups that were formed by local entrepreneurs. Some met monthly and some met weekly. It is great to network with like-minded individuals.

After six months I decided to finally get a website. Once I did that my business exploded. I could do all of the networking I wanted but without a website it was almost useless. I could promote myself because people like to check you out before they hire you. And the fun part was not a lot of people knew what a virtual assistant was, so I liked having a different business that made people wonder if it was viable. I like to be outside the box and follow my own path.

I was starting to get referrals from people who had heard about my business. Jim and I discussed how many clients I would need before I could go full-time with it. We penciled it out. My full-time job was commission-based because I was a mortgage loan officer. It didn't take much money to supersede what I was making there. After nine months of working my business part-time, I had retained three clients and knew the income was steady, so I could quit my full-time job. I named my business SimmonsVirtualAssistant.com.

At first I would take on any clients who would hire me because that was how much I wanted this to succeed. Even if I didn't know how to do the tasks they were asking of me, I employed a "fake it till you make it attitude." I would tell them I did know how and then Google it. That became harder when I had too many clients. But any business can wax and wane. Some clients stay and some go. For the first couple of years I didn't have set hours. I worked as much as I could, depending on the workload. I don't believe in working in my pajamas. Those are for bedtime. I always got up and was at my desk by 8 am. That was my number one rule.

You give up things working a full-time job, plus starting a business and having a family. I would come home, make supper, and go right downstairs to my office and start working. I worked some nights until 9:00 and some nights until midnight, depending on how much work I had to do. But I was willing to do that to benefit myself and my family. I knew that I could go full-time with it and I wouldn't have to work as many hours as I thought.

Once the work was done, I could go have fun with my friends on the weekends; but not until then. They had a hard time understanding, but sometimes sacrifices have to be made in order to start a business. As hard as it was to say no to my friends or my family, it was worth it and it paid off in the end.

The hardest part was saying no to Cody and Jim. I never missed any of Cody's activities but when he wanted me to take him to the mall or something at night, I would have to turn him down if I had something I was working on. Jim was more understanding but would get frustrated if we had something planned and I had to miss it to work. That didn't happen often but when it did, we would reschedule to a more appropriate time. Starting a business involves sacrifice and if you are not willing to, then you are not willing to run your own business.

Starting this business really changed me and how I look at life. When you work for Corporate America or even for the government, you're at their beck and call. You're under their leadership. Now I was free. I could do my own thing. Was I scared? Heck yeah. I was scared to death. Personally, I didn't know what I was doing, yet I knew I was doing the right thing with the virtual assistant work and I was fired up. I looked forward to getting up every day to run my own business. I had never felt this way about a business before.

Once I was fired up, there was no stopping me. It took a lot of time. It took a lot of thinking. I never wrote an official business plan but I kind of had one sketched out. I changed it a lot. I wrote mission statements for my business and what my future goals were. I had a totally different mindset.

Since people didn't know what a virtual assistant was, some thought it was a bogus business. Many people thought I was going to fail and this business would never last. They laughed at me and didn't take me seriously. Little did they know that it was working and it was working very well. There is no greater pleasure than to succeed when others think you are going to fail.

There are times we want quiet and solitude in our lives. While that's nice from time to time, if that's all we have, we could be missing out on something great. If I had sat there and ignored Jean on that plane, I wouldn't be where I am today. I wouldn't have ten years of experience under my belt. Did I want to talk to her? No; I was tired and I just wanted to read my book.

Normally, I'm a very open person. I'll talk to anybody. When you're in business you have to be constantly networking. If you're not promoting your business, then who will?

You've got to open up, even if you're in line at Walmart or the grocery store; tell people what you do. You don't know who those people know. Maybe they don't need your services, but they'll probably know other people who do. I love connecting people. Even if those people can't help your business, maybe you can help them find somebody else. Maybe you can help them connect with somebody who will help them. You should always be giving back to other people.

What a new world you can experience once you open up and learn and meet new people. To me, meeting new people and networking is just exhilarating. I realize some don't like that. Find a way to embrace it and find a way to network. Starting and growing a business requires embracing change; otherwise, you become stagnant.

Take little steps. Change is hard. There were times in my business when I had to fire clients. I remember the first time it happened. I was at the mall on a Saturday afternoon with my mom. It was about 2:00 in the afternoon and this client called me. She said, "Oh my Gosh, Jo. I need it done right now, right now, right now."

I said, "I'm out with my mom. Can it wait a little bit?"

"No, I need this done within the next hour." She was very hard to please and it was getting harder by the day to work with her. But I was still new in my business and wanted to impress her; plus, she gave me a lot of hours and the money was good. But to be honest, she was driving me nuts. Sometimes I avoided her calls because she would just go off.

I said to my mom, "We'd better go back because she wants this done right now."

My mom said, "Really? It's Saturday afternoon."

I told her, "I know, but I have to impress her and I've got to get this done."

I went home and I completed the work. It took me about an hour. I emailed her to let her know it was finished. I didn't hear from her again over the weekend. On Monday, when I went back to work, I called her and said, "Now did you get that information?"

Nonchalantly she said, "Oh yeah. Did you get that done?"

I was furious. "Are you kidding me? I left the mall with my mom. I was spending quality time with my mother, but I got this done for you and you didn't even know I got it done."

She replied, "Oh no, sorry. I didn't realize you were at the mall with your mom."

I said, "Yes you did. I told you that I was there." I was so frustrated and upset that I hung up the phone on her.

I talked with Jim that night. I asked him, "What do I do?"

He said ever so bluntly, "Fire her."

"I've never fired somebody before," I admitted. "I've never fired a client."

He said, "You have to fire her. She is stressing you out."

And I was stressed. My stomach and head hurt. I cried over this client. I was starting to think the good money I was making from her was not worth it. I was getting stressed out even at the thought of firing her, but I was so mad that I knew it was time. She was a referral from a very good client of mine and she herself had been my client for six months. But I knew the time had to come to fire her.

The next day, I set up a time to talk with her. I said, "I'm sorry. I cannot deal with you. I cannot deal with you calling me on the weekends and then not appreciating anything I've done and I'm just not putting up with it anymore." At first she tried talking me into keeping her as a client, but she could tell I was serious. She finally agreed that we could dissolve our working relationship.

Nobody ever taught me how to fire someone. I thought once I fired her, it would end my business, but in retrospect it opened up a whole new world of clients.

I made a new rule for my business that I would no longer work with clients who were difficult like that. I could tell by their attitude and work ethics which ones to avoid. Once I made that change, I opened myself up new and wonderful clients. Once you get rid of the negative, it gives the positive a chance to shine in. I could be more assertive with clients and be open and honest with them. If I didn't think our personalities meshed well together, I told them right away and would refer them to other virtual assistants with whom I thought they would work better. The clients were very appreciative. What a great feeling it was to know I could pick and choose whom I wanted to work with. That's what I love about change.

I live with vitality. I am naturally energetic and a strong female. I get fired up even now, thinking about my virtual assistant business and being able to help other people. If you're working a business where you don't have the vitality, you don't need to be doing that business or something needs to change in that business so you can get that vitality back. Lack of it is going to show your customers that something is missing and you will begin to lose your connections and client base.

Everywhere I went, I told people what I did. Once you do that, you open up new customers, new clients. People will refer you. I did a little advertising for about a year. I never saw a return on my money. After a year I had enough clients who would refer me that I had word of mouth referrals from then on. Those are the best kinds of referrals because people trust people. When I talked to others, they could see I was passionate about my business. Once that happens, it's just awesome. If you can live with vitality, open up with people and explore the world around you. It will be the greatest thing you've ever experienced.

CHAPTER 8
The Diagnosis

JIM WAS working at a regular job when he started getting sicker. I didn't know why and neither did he. He was missing a lot of work and was lacking motivation. He had the same symptoms that he had always had: feeling like he had the flu, headaches, body aches, a slight fever and depression. Except they were getting worse. He was never jaundiced. He was on medicine for depression and had recently been diagnosed with diabetes and high blood pressure. I rationalized that maybe the diabetes was causing the symptoms. After consulting with our family physician, she assured me that was not the case.

Our family doctor ran a bunch of blood tests and frequently checked his liver enzymes. She sat us down and informed us she thought his Hepatitis C was returning. We were still in consultation with Jim's hepatologist in Colorado and upon reviewing the bloodwork, he agreed. The hepatologist told us if Jim didn't get treatment for this, he could end up with full-blown Hepatitis C again, which would eventually become end stage liver disease. Then he would need a liver transplant. I was shocked by all of this. I didn't want him sick so I blocked it from my brain. I wouldn't allow myself to think Jim was that sick. His hepatologist in Colorado ordered a new, improved version of Interferon that might help stop the progression of the disease.

Jim was not thrilled with resuming the injections but I told him to take them and he could be healed. That is how I dealt with things: *just do what you are told and everything will be fine.* We got a month's worth of shots and placed them in the refrigerator as instructed. Jim took two weeks' worth of them, then quit after that. He stated he was done taking them as they were starting to make him sick. He hated that feeling and didn't want to go through what he had when he had taken them in the past. He said he would get severe nausea, vomiting, bad headaches, loose stools, poor appetite and the list continued. I begged him to take them and said I would help him through it and these were supposed to make him better. He refused and said he felt better not taking them than taking them. The package sat in the bottom of the refrigerator. I never threw them out. I was hopeful that one day he would restart them.

Jim continued working but kept calling in sick. Unfortunately, this job didn't put up with it. After the third instance, they called him into the office to fire him. He called me right after to let me know what had happened. When he walked in the front door I met him on the landing. We embraced and hugged for the longest time. We couldn't and wouldn't let each other go. We both cried. It was almost as if we knew something dramatic had just changed in our relationship. Jim was devastated. He was 49 years old and this was the first firing he had experienced. He laid in bed for a week after that, contemplating what he should do. I saw a change in him. His motivation declined and his depression worsened.

Thankfully he could find another job. It was a lot less money and more physically demanding than what he had done before, but he felt a sense of pride since he was providing for his family again. All of this happened in early 2007.

In the interim, we had rented out our Colorado home to friends we trusted. They destroyed the downstairs that we had just renovated at a cost of $15,000, and started paying their rent later than expected. All of this created a financial strain as we struggled to make two house payments without a predictable income. Jim was working but not on a full-time salary. I was working my virtual assistant business full-time and got a part-time job to help make ends meet. I was working practically 24/7 just to build the business, work the part-time job, tend to Jim and raise Cody.

By this time, Jim was starting to let me take over things like the finances, medical appointments, and the overall care of our household and family. He felt bad that I had to go and work a part-time job but in my opinion there was no other choice. My tendency to control things was kicking in and when the going gets tough for me, I tend to "kick into gear." Jim always said from day one that "our marriage is 50/50," but this was getting to be a lot for me to endure. The financial issues alone were causing a lot of stress in our marriage, which also caused a lot of stress on him with his illness.

So it was kind of a double-edged sword; if you're missing work because you're not feeling good, but you have financial issues and marriage issues, that creates a serious situation. We were only into our sixth year of marriage when Cody asked, "What the heck is going on with Jim? Why isn't he working and why is he so sick?"

I tried explaining to Cody about Jim's illness, but he didn't look sick. On the outside he remained muscular, physically fit and had a healthy appearance.

I think that was the hardest part. Hepatitis C is a silent killer. He looked great physically but inside it was a different story. Unfortunately, what you see on the outside is not always what's going on inside. I know everybody's fighting a battle and we just never know what it is. Some make it public and some keep it private. Jim preferred to keep ours private. He never wanted me to tell people what illness he had. He made me swear I would keep it secret and I did. I made up excuses for why he wouldn't come out with our friends. I lied and I hated it. I wanted people to know so they could support us. My family was even wondering what was going on. With the financial issues happening, we consulted attorneys and spoke with investors about our house in Colorado. There were months when I had to decide which house came first - our family home or the one in Colorado. Jim was depressed about the Colorado house because he and his dad had built it. It was his dream home and now the renters were destroying it and we were losing it. We faced one tough decision after another. It wasn't easy. That whole year of 2007 was rough.

Unfortunately, that was also the time of the financial crisis that hit the US. The stock market plunged, then so did the housing market. Big corporations had become corrupt and the whistles were being blown on them. The whole United States was in financial crisis. Normally I can sleep through anything, except this. I would lie awake at night wondering how we were going to pay the next house payment. It got tougher and tougher. I laid awake at night praying for money to come in from somewhere to help make ends meet.

I am so thankful for Jim's best friend Michael. They got to be friends from working together. They were both Navy veterans, so Michael kept pestering Jim to go to the VA and check out specialists there. Jim refused for a year. Somehow, he gave in, and the VA doctors determined right away that he was a sick man. Michael advised him to apply for disability through the VA, and he got approved for 60 percent. With this approval, plus a lump sum of back pay, my prayers were answered. We got some breathing room.

We had two dogs: a yellow lab named Belle who Jim had for years before we met, and a black lab (chosen by Cody) that he named Claire. Jim always considered Belle his baby since he had no other kids besides Cody. She was eleven years old and at the end of September 2007, she started getting sick and we didn't know what was going on. The vet told us she had a small tumor on her hip, which is common to her breed. There wasn't much they could do. Belle got to the point where her hind legs wouldn't move and she was in a lot of pain. It was mid-October and I told Jim it was time to put her to sleep. Cody's birthday was the next day and I didn't want her passing on his birthday. Belle was the first dog Cody had ever had. She was our precious family dog. Before then, I had never had to put a dog to sleep before. As my friend Cindi has said, it is gut-wrenching. I cried for days.

Nothing hit Jim - all the financial issues, the sickness - nothing hit him as hard as putting his beloved Belle to sleep. He was never the same man after Belle died.

I wasn't sure how to approach him some days as his depression was getting worse. He would come home from work and go right to bed. I knew his sickness and grief was robbing him of passion and joy in his life. I was trying to bring as much happiness to it as I could. I kept encouraging him to go do things together. He refused, stating that either we could not afford it or that he didn't feel good. It was usually one or the other. He would dwell on the financial mistakes we had made. I couldn't believe we got ourselves into it either. I knew after my younger years of being a single mom that I never wanted to go through those poverty days again, yet and here I was. Thankfully, with the VA and getting his disability, things were starting to look brighter again. It is nice to have some breathing room after being so desperate for financial happiness.

Through all of these trying times that year, Jim had been in and out of the doctor's office numerous times. They encouraged him to restart the shots but he refused. So they tried other medicines without success. His symptoms were getting worse. The month of November came and he got sicker. He was in and out of the clinics and he kept missing more work until the VA finally admitted him to the hospital. He was admitted the day before Thanksgiving, on Wednesday, November 21, 2007. I was hopeful they could finally figure out what to do with him since it didn't seem like anything else was working. I was also scared and remember thinking back to my childhood when my dad was in the hospital over Thanksgiving and died two and a half weeks later.

It was a stressful Thanksgiving that year. My mother was gone visiting my brother and his family in Utah, for which I was thankful. People were calling, including my mother, wondering what was going on. I didn't know what to tell them as I didn't know myself. I wasn't ready to disclose Jim's secret. The diagnosis of end-stage liver cancer came on Friday, November 23rd. I sat on the side of Jim's bed and just gazed at the doctor. What did this mean?

The doctor proceeded to tell us that Jim needed a liver transplant because his liver was shutting down. He was telling us what to expect and for me it was like a fog was going around him and all I could hear were muffled words. I remember looking at him and he looked like he was in a fog. I tilted my head to the right and then back to the left and tried to listen but my mind wouldn't concentrate on him. All I could think about was, "What are we going to do now?"

It took a couple of minutes with the doctor asking me if I understood what he was saying before I "came to." Once he did, things became clearer again and my brain started concentrating. The doctor looked at me and said Jim would need my support. This was going to a long, tough journey for Jim, but it would be an even tougher journey for me as the caregiver. He looked me directly in the eyes and said, "You are going to need help."

Instinctively my heart and gut kicked into gear as it always does and I told the doctor, "Oh no, I'm going to do this. I'll take care of him. He's my husband. For better for worse, for richer or for poorer, in sickness and in health."

Again the doctor looked me straight in the eye, pointed his finger at me and said, "You are going to need help and you will need to accept it. It might not be now but it will come and you will need help."

Jim and I looked at each other and I thought, *What's going on? What does all this mean? What does end-stage liver disease mean?* The doctor said Jim would need a liver transplant. His liver was shutting down to the point that there was nothing more, medically, they could do. They could treat him with medication for now to help keep him stabilized, but he would need a transplant. He would have to be put on the transplant list.

And my mouth just dropped open. I know they had kind of uttered those words in the past. They'd warned us about it but we dismissed it. They warned us again, and again the warnings were dismissed. This time there was no getting around it. He needed a new liver to live out the rest of his life. If he didn't get one, he would die. All I could think about was my friend Fran in Colorado who had undergone a kidney transplant and was doing great afterward. If she could do it so could Jim; I had faith it was possible. I'm the ultimate positive, optimistic person. I will look at the bright side of every situation. I knew he could beat this.

The doctor stepped out of the room so Jim and I could talk. Jim hadn't said too much and I told him we were going to beat this. We were going to fight this and win. He started getting tears in his eyes and said, "I don't know if I can."

"You have to!" I exclaimed. "We're a family. You have to stay around. You have to fight for your family."

And he said, "I don't know Jo. I don't know if I can do this. I don't know if I'm strong enough." He looked so sad, fragile and defeated. I told him not to give up yet as this was just a diagnosis and not a prognosis. He put his head down, shook his head and said, "I should have taken that medicine back when they gave it to me."

"We can't look at that now," I told him. "We can't look at the past. We have to look at the future and figure out how we're going to beat this and how you're going to get that liver transplant."

The doctors came back in. The three of them looked at both of us and told us we had no idea what we were in for. For a few moments I hated the doctors and but I was also thankful. They tried explaining the fatigue, exhaustion, and pain he would endure as well as the hospitalizations that would happen because of this. There would be time spent away from family. He couldn't work any longer. He would have to undergo months of testing just to be considered for the transplant list. There were no guarantees of being placed on it. No guarantees of a new liver.

The doctors looked at me and said, "Do you understand what we are saying?" I told them I did. I had to be stronger than I'd ever been before. I'd battled other things that had made me stronger. I battled the emotional, financial and physical stress, but this was a whole new category I wasn't prepared for. But I kept smiling and looking at Jim and telling him everything would be alright and we would fight this. I told myself to remain positive, keep smiling and don't cry.

The main doctor looked at me and asked to see me in the hallway. I excused myself from Jim's room and I stepped outside. He looked at me and he stated he didn't think I truly understood what I was in for. He wanted to know if I had family and friends who could help.

I looked at him and I said, "Well, yeah, I'm pretty sure people will help." I couldn't guarantee that 100 percent, though, as everyone had their own families to care for.

The doctor put his hands on my shoulders, grasped them kind of tightly and said, "You cannot do this alone. You are going to need help because he is going to get a lot sicker before he gets better. If he is approved for a transplant he will be near death before it is done." I now treasured him since he cared so much about the both of us. I knew at that moment this was serious and we were in for the long haul. There was no more laughing about it and we were no longer in control of Jim's health; it controlled us.

I promised him I would do that. I promised him that I would go out of my way to do what was right for me so I'd be strong enough to fight for Jim. "You have to take care of yourself. You are going to be a caregiver to a very, very sick man, and you have to take care of yourself." As I gulped back my fear of the future, I promised the doctor I would do that.

Our first transition into learning about liver transplants involved letting the VA know where we wanted to have it done. Since the VA in Sioux Falls did not do them nor did any place in South Dakota, we had our option of either going to the VA in Portland, Oregon or Pittsburgh, Pennsylvania to have the actual surgery. Now I was getting scared. He couldn't even have the transplant in our home state. Who would come to help? How would we do this? Our heads were spinning but they needed to know which place we wanted to go. Jim was big into football and loved the Broncos. We joked around and reasoned since Oregon didn't have a pro football team and Pittsburgh did that he would go to Pittsburgh. We tried to make light of little things as we knew our battle had just begun. He was set up with a transplant coordinator at the VA in Sioux Falls and one at the Pittsburgh VA. They would coordinate all of his testing and they were our future at that point.

While Jim was still in the hospital, family and friends were calling asking what was going on with him. I finally had to let his secret out that he had Hepatitis C and he didn't want anyone to know about it. It was hard telling my friends because I hated secrets and lying and now I had to be honest and tell them why I kept it a secret. Some were disappointed while others were encouraging. My mother had called from Utah wondering what was going on, and I had to tell her too. People thought they could contract Hepatitis C from Jim and were concerned about that. I told them it would be rare for that to happen and it had to be blood on blood contact. I could tell by their reactions they were thinking back, trying to remember if that had ever happened. Was I concerned about it? Yes, I was for both Cody and me. But I knew it had never happened. I had made sure of that through the years. I always kept a watchful eye and if Jim was bleeding I made him put a band aid on right away and no one was to touch it except him.

I asked my family and friends to pray for us. That was a big step for me, since I didn't like people thinking less of us. I felt like I had a persona to keep up and this brought me back down to my core. I wanted to be the one praying for others, not the one being prayed for. Jim's secret was out. What would people think of us? My vulnerability was very visible. Why did I care what they thought? But I did. I felt sorry for myself and thought *here I go again*. First it was Cody's dad and me divorcing, then being a single mom and now having a sick husband. Lord, what else would come my way? Jim and I were a happily married couple. We loved each other and had a loving family. I wanted Jim healed and our home to be the same as it had been or better. I wanted 2007 to end and never look back.

Having a sickness is hard. Hard when you know death will come without a transplant. Jim never talked of death. All he ever said about it was, "You guys will be taken care of," which meant we had both had life insurance policies. I didn't want to talk death either. Nor did I want the life insurance money. I wanted him to be well. We don't always get what we want.

A wonderful benefit of having your own business and working from home is being able to schedule clients around doctor's appointments. From that perspective, it is wonderful to be your own boss. I loved my business and it gave me the drive and desire to get up every day and work harder at it than I did the day before. I would get lost in my work and I felt it was the best medicine for me at the time. I escaped from the pain of the problems by working.

From a financial perspective, it is tough because you have only yourself to count on to bring in the income. When you miss work, you miss out on money. There is no overtime pay, sick or vacation pay. Need extra income coming in? Get a part-time job or find things to sell on Craigslist or eBay. Set up a PayPal account, Craigslist and eBay account and start selling. It helps declutter the home and brings in extra income. This way you have the financial resources to handle things when you have slow times in your business or there is a personal or medical issue that comes up.

When you are self-employed, issues are going to arise no matter what. Talk to people who you trust. Talk to a confidant. Go have coffee with somebody. Even if it is just to get out of the house for a little bit. I did that a lot. I would go schedule an hour with a friend or business consultant and have coffee. It was a great breakaway from my business and gave me a fresh start and different ideas. Schedule a lunch or go to a networking meeting, something to get your mind away from things. That will help you grow personally as well as in your business, which will aid you as you tackle different issues.

When a crisis does occur, deal with it head-on. Don't procrastinate. We all know what happens when we do; the obstacle just gets bigger and doesn't go away. This happened with Jim's health and it also happened in my business. If things were piling up on me and I didn't want to deal with them, I put them aside and hoped they would go away. They never did. The best thing I learned was to take care of an issue right away because I would sit and worry about it until something did happen. If I don't deal with something head-on, I will stew about it and my stomach will get upset. I won't eat and I'll pay for it health-wise. If I deal with it right away and get it taken care of, I can move on to the next project. And if it means I have to put in longer hours to get it done, I'll do it because it's important to the client; it's important to me, and it's important to getting the work done.

What helped me the most was writing down the pros and cons of the crisis. I would ask myself, *Will this affect my business in a negative way? What is the worst that can come of this? How do I rectify it as soon as possible?* If you can answer these questions in a timely fashion, the crisis will soon dissipate and you will come out a better business person because of it. As my mother always says, "This too shall pass," and it always has.

Through anything in life, remember to live, laugh and love. I smile and laugh all the time, especially through crises. It might not be right but it is how I handle them. That is why the doctor kept looking at me and needed to talk to me out in the hallway. He didn't think I took it seriously because I wasn't crying. People say to me all the time that they cannot believe how I always have a happy face on. I always seem happy. I choose to be happy. I chose that reaction early on in my adult life. I don't know any other way.

I am glad that people didn't know the depth of the pain that was underneath and the fear of the unknown that I felt. Only a select few knew how scared I was. I didn't want people thinking Jim was going to die. I wouldn't allow myself to think it. This attitude works for business as well. I bragged up my business even when I didn't have business. I did the "fake it till you make it" scenario. I loved my business so much that everywhere I went, people knew it. Life is an adventure and we never know what the next day will bring. So live it, love it and endure it.

When you're having a hard time, give back to others. I've relied on the Lord through my life for strength and guidance. When helping others, our burdens seem lessened. To me, giving back to others is love. When Jim became sick I started going to kickboxing to relieve stress. There were days when I wanted to scream and cry, and I did that too. But on an everyday basis there was nothing better than hitting that bag and getting the frustrations out. I would help others who were new to the sport. It felt good. I got lost in the moment and my stress was relieved by helping someone else. I did the same thing when someone I knew wanted to start a new business. They would call me up and ask me questions. I felt honored they would do that. Giving back is in fact giving love to God.

Surely God is my salvation; I will trust and not be afraid. The Lord,
the Lord, is my strength and my song; he has become my salvation.
(Isaiah 12:2)

CHAPTER 9
Jim's Passing and Grief

AFTER JIM was diagnosed in November 2007, our lives were a roller coaster ride; we never knew what the next day would bring. He was in and out of the hospital often. But nothing prepared us for the year between August 2009 and July 2010, when he was in the hospital at least a week out of every month. That was also the year Cody was a senior in high school.

Among the neat things about Jim and Cody was their closeness, which included Jim teaching Cody how to play football when he was nine years old. He was the first one to teach my son how to throw a football and how to play the game. Jim even coached Cody's sixth grade baseball team. Cody went on to play high school football and was a starter on the varsity squad. Jim wasn't able to watch all the games because of his sickness, but thankfully the games were announced on the radio. If he could not go to a game, he would sit and listen to it. I thought it was cute that my mom would do the same at her house if she couldn't get to the game. Then if they heard Cody's name announced they would call each other and talk about the plays because Cody was such a good player.

Cody's senior year was also the worst year for Jim's sickness. Thankfully Jim did make it to two of Cody's football games. The first one was the homecoming game. Cody was on the homecoming royalty court so the parents were asked to be on the field with their players at the beginning of the game while the court was announced. Both Jim and I were so proud of Cody and all of his accomplishments. Jim had been released from the hospital, after a week's stay, the day before the game and he said he would make it to that game and stand next to him. And he did. It was a proud moment for all of us as a family.

For the last game of Cody's high school career, I was a mess. I was sad because it was his last game and I was scared of what the future would hold, both for Cody since he was a senior, and for our family. I think I knew instinctively that things were going to change. We were playing in another city at a semi-final game. If we won that game, we would go to the championship, but I knew our chances were slim. We were playing one of the largest schools in the state. It was a beautiful day in October but it was really windy. Jim had been out of the hospital that time for about a week. He felt good and wanted to go to the game. I was only thinking of myself, since this was my baby's last game of his high school career. My mom also accompanied us to the game. The wind was too much for her. With her vision problems the wind was causing her eyes to water so badly she wanted to go to the car and listen to the game. I asked Jim if he would go sit with her in the car since I was not leaving. Being the kind, considerate man he was, he said yes. At halftime, I walked them both to the car. I returned to my seat and they listened to the rest of the game on the radio.

That was the good part about 2009. The worst part is life can throw you curve balls, and I have learned that how you deal with them is what makes you who you are. A divorce is devastating but to watch a loved one become sicker and sicker when there's nothing you can do about it is about as gut wrenching as it becomes.

Jim's illness required a miracle liver transplant and without it his death was imminent. Living with that knowledge, day in and day out, was devastating. I'm not sure Jim fully understood that. He was on fourteen medications which were affecting his memory and thought processes, so it was becoming harder for him to comprehend things. One thing Jim would say a lot was that he wanted to "go home." The first time I heard it I said, "You are home."

He said, "No, I mean home in Heaven."

I'd say, "You're not doing it under my watch today. We're going to keep a positive attitude, we're going to keep going, and we're going to keep fighting." I look back now and see how he was slowly slipping away and I was desperately trying to hold on. I give that man so much credit for fighting as long as he did as sick as he was. It could not have been easy for him.

I searched for answers to Jim's illness. I wanted straight facts. We had so many doctors that it was hard for any of them to get to know Jim and some only told me what I wanted to hear. Then God answered my prayer: In early 2009, Jim was reassigned to a wonderful doctor. He was open and honest with us and that was exactly what I needed. He knew about liver transplants and was an advocate for Jim and me. In March 2009, he was straight with us. He said, "Look, most people who need liver transplants only live two-and-a-half to three years."

All of a sudden, it felt like someone had punched me in the gut. I sat there and trembled. "What are you talking about? He's going to get a liver!"

The doctor in his calm demeanor looked me in the eyes and said again, "If he doesn't, most people only live two-and-a-half to three years."

I thought, *Oh, my God, that's only another one to one-and-a-half years from now. What am I going to do?* Jim sat there expressionless. I'm not sure he fully understood what was going on. He then looked at me with those beautiful blue eyes and a blank stare, and being the eternal optimist I said, "We're going to fight this."

With end-stage liver disease, sometimes the patients can develop what is known as hepatic encephalopathy, which means the brain becomes enlarged if the ammonia levels in the blood get too high. This happened quite frequently with him and this was the main reason for his hospitalizations. Once he was hospitalized they would give him large doses of Lactulose, the medicine to help bring the ammonia levels down. It comes with nasty side effects and the person taking it has to be close to a bathroom usually at all times. I felt so bad for him, as he would have bathroom accidents and couldn't control his bowel movements.

There were many days I was monitoring how much and when he took his medicine in order to make sure he got the right dosage every time. He wanted to try and still be independent and I had to honor that but still wanted to be sure he took his meds. I knew him so well through this illness that I could tell how much medicine he had taken by how he was acting. I could recite it all to the doctors when we had to go to the ER. It got to be a very familiar pattern.

According to Healthgrades.com, Ammonia is a nitrogen waste compound that is normally excreted in the urine. An elevated blood ammonia level is an excessive accumulation of ammonia in the blood. An elevated blood ammonia level occurs when the kidneys or liver are not working properly, allowing waste to remain in the bloodstream.

While Cody was in high school, I always tried to make things normal for him, as much as normal could be. He would come home from school and I guess maybe I tried hiding Jim's illness from him. I didn't know how bad it would be, but maybe I was just in pure denial. Cody would come home from school, walk in the front door and first thing he would ask is, "Where's Jim?"

I'd say, "He's in the hospital again." I hated having to tell him that. I looked forward to the days when he would come home from school and ask where Jim was and I could say watching TV or outside. It made me feel whole again knowing we were all under the same roof…even if it was only for a short time.

Cody was smarter than I gave him credit for, because he knew the intensity of Jim's illness. Like I said, maybe I was in denial, but I always tried to make it look like it was better than what it was. Our friends would ask, "How's Jim?"

I would say, "He's fine." But inside I was screaming, *Why don't you just come see for yourself? Why don't you come say hi to him? Or better yet, why not ask how I am doing?* I was suffering too and in my mind no one seemed to care about me. The caregiver often gets left out since everyone is so focused on the sick person. There were people who checked up on me daily and when they did ask how I was doing I usually responded with "fine." I began to realize what the doctor meant when he said I would need help.

Jim closed people off. He didn't want people over and seeing him the way he was. But I also think people get scared. They don't know what to do or say in times like these. Unless you have gone through it yourself, it can be hard. I think they are afraid that they will get whatever the sick person has. Toward the end, I had multiple people ask if they could help me but I wouldn't let them. I figured if people didn't know the depth of our pain then it would go away, and eventually it did, but not in the way that I wanted.

Jim always considered me his nurse and would call me that frequently. I didn't want to be his nurse; I wanted to be his wife. I didn't want to be the person who had to take care of him all the time. I wanted my husband back. I wanted the man I danced together with and held hands with in the kitchen while making supper together, the man I would just lie in bed with and talk about everything, or look up at the stars with and talk about the beautiful night. I wanted the man back who got us to move to South Dakota, said I would have the house that I wanted, and was a wonderful dad to my son. I wanted that man back.

We don't always get what we want. God might have different plans. When we took our wedding vows, I vowed to care for Jim in sickness and in health, and I meant it. The roller coaster ride comes when the sick spouse is feeling better and wants to go do things, then you go back into the wife role. When the illness takes back over, then you are back to playing nurse. It was a vicious cycle for us.

Jim enjoyed date nights. We had one every month. Toward the end our date night was just going out for supper. But that was enough and it got us out of the house. When we had date nights, I liked being the wife again. Each time he wanted one, I got my hopes up that maybe things were turning for the better. False hope... but still hope. Our last family outing was at the beginning of March 2010 when

Cody, Jim and I went out for supper. Our original plan was supper and a semi-pro basketball game, but we ended up going later than expected so we just had supper. While at a Chinese restaurant, the three of us sat and talked and laughed like we had no worries. It was a night I'll never forget. Jim was admitted to the hospital two weeks later and didn't come home again except for Cody's graduation.

Cody graduated in May 2010. Graduation was hard for me as I knew I would become an empty nester after he left for college in the fall. I wanted to cry at the thought of Cody leaving but I was busy getting everything ready for the graduation party that we shared with another family. I wanted everything to be perfect. I knew my life was changing in a big way and yet I didn't want to fully accept it.

Thankfully, Jim could come home from the hospital that weekend. He was sick, but wanted to be home for graduation. When I picked him up he looked frail and weak. I clung to the hope that he would have his transplant in the near future. That hope kept me going. Jim was very close to his dad, who now suffered from dementia. His dad and stepmom came to visit, but both men were too ill to make it to the ceremony. Instead they sat in the living room and talked all afternoon long. It was precious seeing them together.

What a blessing that those two could spend that quality time together on that Saturday and Sunday. Jim's parents left on Sunday afternoon and Jim went to bed. He hated seeing his dad leave. By Monday, Jim was so sick that I had to get him back to the hospital. He was not able to walk and needed a wheelchair to get inside. He was so sick, but I was happy he could be home for the joyous weekend. As I wheeled him into the hospital where he was staying, I just had that heartbreaking feeling he wasn't coming home again. I started shaking and crying but wouldn't let him see me. I'm not sure how I pulled that off, but I did.

Back when Cody was about five, we had found out from a dentist that something was wrong with his jaw. He sent us to an orthodontist who confirmed he would need jaw surgery when he got older to correct an extreme under-bite. The surgery required both jaws to be broken and realigned. It had to wait, however, until he was done growing. They took x-rays of his hands while he was in eighth grade and again as a junior in high school. By his junior year he had stopped growing so Cody decided he wanted to do the surgery before he left for college.

The first round was getting braces on. That was preparing him for surgery which we aimed for a month after graduation in June 2010. The grueling part of this surgery was that he had to have both jaws broken, the bottom jaw pushed back, and the top jaw pushed forward. It didn't sound fun but Cody was ready to endure it to "get it over with" before he started college. Unfortunately, with this type of surgery, he had to see a specialized surgeon and we were sent to the University of Nebraska at Omaha, which is a three-hour drive each way. This was a work in progress and numerous trips to Omaha had already taken place. Surgery was scheduled for June 17, 2010.

Cody and I went down for it. Jim's health was rapidly declining and he was still at the VA hospital in Sioux Falls at the same time. Jim knew that Cody had to have this surgery and was very concerned for him. When we were down there, Jim called on the day of the surgery and asked how he was doing. Since he couldn't talk very well, he had the nurse call two or three times checking in on Cody. The nurse told me that Jim was persistent and wanted to call every chance he could. How sweet is that?

Cody had to spend the night in the hospital and I stayed too. I brought Cody home the next day. I felt so sorry for him. He was wrapped in ice bandages the whole way around his head. It was not a pretty sight, but the doctor told us it had to get ugly before it got better. The surgery had gone well and the doctor was pleased. That was on Friday. I spent the days and nights waiting on Cody since he was in a lot of pain and needed much help.

On Sunday, which was Father's Day, I broke away for about two hours to go see Jim, who had been stable until I got up there to see him. When I entered I heard a strange noise. He was gasping for breath. As I approached his eyes rolled to the back of his head. His chest would arch up and his head tilt back. The gasping was the worst sound I had ever heard. I called for a nurse and no one heard me. I frantically started punching the nurse call button.

When the nurses finally arrived they called for the doctors to come stat. I knew that wasn't good. They got his breathing regulated and once he was stabilized, he was moved to ICU. That was the first time my brain would let me think that maybe he was going to die. I cried. I couldn't believe he was so close to dying at that moment. I was so scared when I found him in that state. I yelled at the nurses. The male nurse confirmed he had just seen him ten minutes earlier and he wasn't like that. I didn't care, as he was like that when I arrived. My heart sank and felt heavy. My life was so crazy with Cody's surgery, and now Jim almost dying, all within a five-minute time-frame I thought I had lost everybody. The stress of life was finally starting to hit me.

When Jim came to after being placed in ICU, he reached for my hand and I put my right hand out to reach his. He whispered the best he could, "You saved my life. See, you are my nurse." The funny thing was, when I was in college I always wanted to be a nurse but I never wanted to do all of that studying.

I didn't know what to say because I was thinking *Yes, I saved your life, and I will always save your life no matter what.* I winked at him, smiled, and jokingly said, "You owe me now."

He whispered, "I'll always owe you."

I said, "No, we don't owe each other anything. We're married; this is what married couples do. We take care of each other."

As bad as that was, it was nothing compared to what was coming. Jim's birthday was the next week, on June 24th. He turned fifty-three that day. In the morning, I got a call from our Sioux Falls VA transplant coordinator. She informed us that since Jim's condition had worsened he was now placed higher on the liver transplant list. She said, "Jim you're getting your birthday present. You're going to Pittsburgh."

Both Jim and I were excited. Petrified, but excited, as I knew he would be getting his new liver soon. My emotions were going all over the place; I was so excited that he was sick enough to get a transplant but mad at myself for being excited about that. When you are in a situation like this you have to be happy for the things that are going to make it better. Getting sicker was going to be making it better.

In 2007, when he was diagnosed, he went through a battery of tests that took months to perform. Our transplant coordinator in Sioux Falls was under the direction of the VA liver transplant coordinator from Pittsburgh. We were also under their direction in terms of what tests needed to be performed. Yet all of the tests were performed in Sioux Falls at the VA. It was a difficult and frustrating process. They denied Jim at first, stating his heart wasn't strong enough. I kept fighting that because it was ridiculous. As strong and muscular as he was, I knew his heart was in good condition. Finally, after several other heart tests, they decided he was a candidate. It took a full year for him to be placed on the list.

When you are placed on the liver transplant list you are assigned a number. That number correlates with how sick you are. Jim was always ranked from twelve to fourteen. It was frustrating. He was close a couple of times, ranking up to twenty-two, but then would get better so his score was lowered again. To be considered in imminent danger and placed high on the transplant list your score must be twenty-four to twenty-five. On Jim's birthday, they ranked him a twenty-four and he was transferred to Pittsburgh. I was told by several doctors you practically have to be dead before you get a transplant and now I believed them.

Six months earlier, in January of 2010, he was in the hospital and was very sick. I called our transplant coordinator in Pittsburgh, begging her to transfer him. Our Sioux Falls coordinator was also in touch with Pittsburgh but there was no response while he was hospitalized. I felt from the get-go that they had dragged their feet since he was a very sick man. Thankfully, Sioux Falls got him stabilized and he was starting to feel better. Since we had not heard from Pittsburgh and Jim was feeling better, he wanted to go home. I asked him to stay one more day and he refused. The doctors decided to release him. I felt a sense of discouragement. We were home a couple of days when the call from the VA transplant coordinator in Pittsburgh came. She said, "I'm sorry I didn't get your call sooner. If he had remained in the hospital, we would have transferred him."

My heart sank. I was speechless for a moment. I started crying and asking her over and over, "Why didn't you call me back two days ago when he was still there?"

It's such a frustrating system. They told us the liver is the hardest organ to receive. Which to me is frustrating since you can take a piece of someone else's liver and use it. But I'm no doctor; just a wife who wanted her husband well.

When Jim was transferred to Pittsburgh, I tried getting some of his family to go out and be with him since I had to stay back with Cody and get an infection under control. Jim has one sister who at first said she and her husband would go stay with him, then at the last minute she backed out due to her own medical conditions. Jim's dad couldn't go and he didn't want his mom going due to her alcoholism. I was in a quandary.

Unfortunately, he was out there for about a week by himself but they took good care of him and I was in daily, actually almost hourly, contact with them to make sure everything was going okay. I talked his friend Michael from Colorado into going with me out there. I said I just felt like I needed somebody out there with me to be my right-hand person and he agreed. Michael's girlfriend was a gem. Even though she knew it would be hard on him, she picked up the pieces after he got home. I would have been lost without them.

I got Cody stabilized; he felt okay to stay on his own after the infection was over and he was able to eat a little bit again. Because it was major jaw surgery, he wasn't able to eat anything. He was only able to drink liquid and he had a hard time breathing because his nose was all stuffed up; it was a mess.

I finally got him stabilized and had my friends come over and check up on him and help grind up his food to eat. Then Michael and I made the long trip to Pittsburgh. When I got to the hospital, Jim was no longer talking. But when he saw me his eyes lit up. His big baby blue eyes glistened like I had never seen them glisten before. He followed me with his eyes and I kept telling him, "I'm here baby, I'm here." I squeezed his hand and hugged him. He tried his best to hug me back but his body was almost limp. I knew something drastic was wrong with him as he wasn't responding to anyone anymore. When he first was flown out there he could talk a little bit, but now nothing. The doctors didn't have any answers for me.

We kept plugging along and I stayed by his side. His room was in the ICU and it was a cold room with a cold floor. It was mid-July and I was cold. I felt the whole hospital was cold. Everyone there loved their beloved Pittsburgh Steelers and I was beginning to hate them. To me it seemed like they cared more for the Steelers than they did for my husband. I know that isn't true, but when they couldn't find answers to my questions, I was very frustrated and wanted to hate all of them and the things they loved. I felt like a fish out of water. We were from South Dakota and all these people were from Pennsylvania. I got more answers out of the nurses than I did the doctors.

What made me the angriest was when I was sitting at Jim's bedside and I saw one of his doctors playing on the internet. The nurse's station was right outside his room. I asked the nurse, "Why isn't he looking into finding a new liver?"

She said, "He has been, but now he is playing on the internet. That is what he does when he is bored."

I thought, *Bored? My husband is dying and he is bored?* "Why the hell isn't he in here transplanting my husband? He should be in here transplanting him instead of just sitting there playing on the computer." I was so mad at him, I wanted to go shake him and tell him to go find Jim a new liver now.

After we had been there a couple of days, Jim just wasn't progressing. The doctor said he was up next on the transplant list, but he wasn't progressing enough to the point where they could perform the surgery. He wasn't talking and they couldn't figure out why.

That Saturday, July 10, 2010, the doctors did an MRI. I was out taking a walk and they called me on my cell phone. "We're so sorry, but the MRI showed there is no brainwave activity left. He's not going to get his transplant and he is going to die soon - within a day or two."

Thankfully Michael was with me because I almost passed out. I started crying and said "What? What do you mean? We're out here so he gets his transplant." Since Jim's main symptom through this whole disease was high ammonia levels, I guess they finally took their toll on his health. I could see where he wouldn't have any brainwave activity but I just couldn't accept it.

In the meantime, as I was talking to the doctor, Cody kept beeping in on my cell phone. He must have known something was going on. I said, "I've got to go. I've got to call my son; I've got to tell him. I just have to tell him."

The doctor said, "When you've done that, come back. We need to talk."

Before we went back to the hospital I made the dreaded call to Cody. I had to tell him the man he considered his dad would not live much longer. I called Cody and I was crying and he said, "Mom, just tell me the truth. You haven't told me the truth at all during any of this. I just want to know the truth."

I said, "I have told you the truth, from what I know. I didn't know what the illness was going to bring. I didn't know, I didn't know." That was one of the worst things I ever had to do. Cody was home, recovering from the surgery, and I was out there with Jim, and I wanted so badly just to go home and hug Cody and just tell him everything was going to be okay. But I couldn't. Now he was home alone, devastated by the news and I was in Pittsburgh, a town I now hated. I told Cody to surround himself with his friends and he did. He has truly amazing friends. I felt so blessed they could be with him when I couldn't.

Michael and I went back to the hospital where the doctors were waiting to talk to me. The doctor said to me, "I'm so sorry. We should have probably done the MRI a day or two ago but there's just no brainwave activity. Even if we transplanted him his brain activity would not come back."

Michael and his girlfriend back in Colorado were true blessings. Because while he was keeping me sane, she was keeping him sane, which is a true gift. She was an angel in disguise through all of this. As we went back and we were standing by Jim's bedside, the doctor said, "If we just could have had him out here six months earlier, maybe we could have saved him."

I stopped him right there and said, "What are you talking about? I was calling, I was begging with the transplant coordinator to get him out here."

I'll never forget his next words, "Unfortunately, he's one of those veterans who fell through the cracks."

I just fell back on Jim's bed and said, "I cannot believe you just said that to me. I cannot believe all the times I've called and I begged, begged, and begged the transplant coordinator to get him out here and you're telling me that he's one of those who fell through the cracks?"

He just said, "I am so sorry. But at this point, there's nothing more we can do," and he walked away.

I was devastated. All this hard work. I told Jim I would never forsake him, I would never stop fighting for him, and I felt like I let him down. I felt like I didn't fight hard enough for him. I was numb…I couldn't think. I couldn't comprehend what they had just said.

After I calmed down and the crying had lessened, the doctor came back in. He said frankly, "We need to have a team meeting tomorrow and figure out what we're going to do with him. Will he die here or do you want to send him back to South Dakota to die?"

How do you answer that? I didn't even know what to say or how to say it. I'm not sure how it came out of my mouth, but I got my thoughts together and said I wanted him back in South Dakota to die. I hated Pittsburgh so much by now and I wanted out of there. I was determined he would not die there. On Sunday, we met with the team of doctors. Jim was very unstable and they were not sure he could travel, but I said he would travel and he would make it back to South Dakota. I wanted his family and friends to come say goodbye to him. I knew in my heart he would make it back just fine.

On Tuesday, July 13th, we all made the trip home to South Dakota. Jim was flown on a medical ambulance airplane and Michael and I took a commercial flight. Once he arrived back at the Sioux Falls VA, he was placed in ICU on life support. I got a plane ticket for his mom to come see him. She was not able to come till Friday night. I was now having to tell people come right away to see him or they could be too late. I couldn't believe those words were coming out of my mouth, but reality had set in and I knew death was imminent. I told his mom Friday might be too late but that was what she chose. Friday at noon the doctor called me into his room. She informed me that it was time to unhook Jim from life support.

I said, "You can't. His mom is flying in at 8:00 tonight, we have to keep him alive."

She said, "I'm sorry, it's time. We have to let him go."

I thought did everybody want him dead? Why couldn't they keep him alive until his mother came into town?

A male nurse spoke gently to me. "Your husband is with the angels now and they are just waiting for their cue to take him home to Heaven."

At that moment I had a peace come over me because Jim used to always say, "I just want to go home to Heaven." I nodded my head in acknowledgement and knew he was right.

They unhooked him from life support around 12:30, but surprisingly he didn't die right away. I thought, *Good for you honey! Keep fighting!* Numerous times I would get really close and talk to him. I kissed his forehead gently and told him how much I loved him. I thanked him for being such a great husband to me and a great dad to Cody. After they removed life support, I got really close to him again and said, "Please hold on because your mom is coming and she wants to see you. After that, you can let go and go be with God and your family and friends who went before you."

Jim's mom's flight got in at 8:00 pm and I went to pick her up. I warned her that he didn't look the same and it would be hard to see him. Neither she nor any of my other friends or family who came to see him were prepared for how he looked. Evelyn got to the hospital room and when she saw him, she screamed, "My baby, my baby boy, oh my God!" She crawled in bed with him and was kissing his forehead and face. She placed her hands all over his chest, placing them on top of the butterfly tattoo that caused all of this pain. She then laid her head on his chest. She held him tightly. I wept like I had never wept before. I felt the depth of her pain since I, too, had a son who I adored.

One thing a nurse told me was that I shouldn't be in the room when he passed. Due to Jim's esophageal varices and his other internal problems, he could spit blood all over when he passed. Since he had Hepatitis C, she didn't want me coming into contact with the blood. But how would I know when he died? Only God knows when it is time to take us home.

I was afraid of seeing someone die so I was okay with it. Plus, I knew for my safety I needed to stay away. My good friend Michele would keep vigil over Jim when I couldn't be there and she was okay seeing death. I was afraid of it since I had never seen it, but yet I didn't want to leave him. The nurses came to me and said, "Our suggestion is go home, get some sleep and we will call you if anything changes or he passes."

Around midnight we left his room. I kissed his forehead gently and said, "It's okay; you can let go now. Your mom has seen you; we've all seen you, we love you and want you to be pain free. You are free to go." My friends and family all came to see him and hung out with us at the hospital as much as they could.

Of course I didn't sleep all night; I kept calling up there to check on him. Eventually I fell asleep and didn't wake up till about 8:30 am. When I woke up I was so anxious and stressed I didn't know what to do. I couldn't think, I couldn't eat; I didn't think I could drive myself to the hospital. Everyone else in the house was sleeping. The phone rang at 9:15 am and I just knew. It was the doctor calling to tell me that at 9:00 am, Jim died peacefully. Nothing violent, just a quiet passing. I was relieved but yet so sad. The date was July 17, 2010. He passed away one day before my forty-third birthday. Death is raw and real. Nothing is as final as death and the grief in that moment overcame me like a knife stabbing my heart over and over again. But in the same sense I was happy for Jim as he was finally at peace and no longer suffering from such a nasty illness. He got his wish; to go home.

Because at the end, he wasn't the man I married; he was just a shell. I knew he didn't want to live like that, and I knew it wasn't the person he wanted to be. Even though I'm the eternal optimist, I finally had to face reality. The reality of death hit me hard. The one thing I never wanted was for Cody to lose a parent like I lost my dad at such a young age; but unfortunately it happened.

The first person I told was Cody. I woke him up and we hugged and cried. Then next was Jim's mom, then Michael who was staying with us too. Next I called my mother. We all cried together.

The hospital told me I needed to go there right away and find a funeral home. Really? I have to deal with all of this now? Can't I just be with my family and friends instead of dealing with this? But the VA was adamant that I pick one right away. I never had even thought of a funeral home through all of Jim's illness. That was the last thing I wanted to do.

When the man from the funeral home arrived at the VA and said he was sorry for my loss, I wanted to say to him, *No you're not. You're happy he passed so you can get my money for the funeral. That's how you operate.* Instead I just said, "Thank you," because I was too numb to say anything else.

Jim had told me he wanted to be cremated so I relayed this to the funeral director. He said we all needed to meet at the funeral home. I told him I would not go to their facility in Sioux Falls, as that was where my dad had been. Memories came flooding back to me of his death and having to go through that grief again. Although I had lost other family members who went through that same funeral home, for some reason this was different. This was personal and I didn't want any part of it.

We opted for their funeral home that was in my town and it was new and very nice. Once we met there we were all sitting around a table talking with the funeral director. He was asking questions like, "What was your husband's full name?"

Before I could say it, Jim's mom said, "Bradley James".

I looked at her in disgust and said, "No, it's not; it's James Bradley. You named him, you should know."

She said, "No, it is Bradley James. Check the birth certificate. I said I have the birth certificate and it says James Bradley. She laughed it off and said, "Oh, well, I'm a drunk; what do I know?"

I couldn't believe what I was hearing. I rolled my eyes and looked at my other friends and family there. The funeral director looked at me in amazement. I said, "It's James Bradley. I have his birth certificate."

So this is how it was going to go. I actually didn't want to go through with a funeral or church service and Jim had never expressed he wanted that either. Family and friends encouraged me to have one for closure so I did.

The next day was my birthday and I didn't want to deal with any of this. Jim and I both loved our birthdays so much! I celebrate mine all month of July. I knew he would have never wanted to pass on my birthday nor would he want me to do any of this planning on that day. So I didn't. I told everybody, "I'm not going to do a thing. Jim would not want me to." They all understood.

At the beginning of July, my washing machine had broken down. My friends decided I should go look for a washing machine on my birthday and I agreed. I never realized how much grief takes out of you. I practically passed out when I was in Home Depot.

The funeral home called on Monday and said I needed to come in and pick out an urn. The only place they had them was at the old building and that was the one place I did not want to go. I tried to get a few people to go with me but they were all busy doing other things. My anxiety was at top level when I walked into the place. I thought I was going to be sick to my stomach and pass out. I wanted to run out of there. I told the director to make it fast as I was going to get sick. He agreed and we went through them.

"Does it really matter since his ashes will be sprinkled in Colorado?"

"Not really," he said. "It all depends on what you want."

I picked one out and I got out of there as fast as I could. My best friend, Dawn, who was with me through this whole process, felt so bad she couldn't come with me. She had lost her husband years earlier and knew how hard that part of it was. She was my rock.

We held the funeral on Wednesday, July 21st. Many people came. I wanted Cody and me to go down the aisle of the church first, just as we did on our wedding day. As we were going to enter the sanctuary of the church, I put my arm in his arm and he grabbed it and said, "Are you ready to go, Mom?"

No, I really wasn't. I didn't want this to start or end but knew I had to get through it to move on. Again, I wanted to turn around and run but I couldn't. So instead I said, "Yep, I guess." Down the aisle we walked. In the church pew, Cody was on one side of me and Jim's dad and stepmom were on the other side. As I do to avoid attention on me, I was making sure everyone else was okay during the service. I kept checking on Cody and Jim's parents. The service was beautiful and the pastor did such an amazing job.

There were people for the service and in some ways I hated seeing them. In other ways, I took comfort in seeing them and I was very grateful for their presence. The one thing that I had told Cody through the years was that when my dad died, I remembered people, lots of people at my house and as much as I hated it, I also took comfort in it. When I had a lot of people at my house after Jim died, I noticed Cody going down to his room and secluding himself. I did the same thing when my dad died. So I would go down and make sure he was okay, but also have him included in the funeral arrangements. My mom did the same with me and I believe that is all part of the grief and healing process.

The week after Jim's passing, Cody and I made a venture up to Colorado and met up with Faith, who had introduced Jim and me. She, her boys, Cody and I found the perfect spot to spread his ashes. Jim loved the water. So we found a spot fitting for him. It was a gorgeous Colorado day and it was a very serene, peaceful feeling when his ashes were spread. I felt so blessed and so humbled. We said our goodbyes for the last time as I fulfilled my promise to him and our life together.

After we got home from Colorado, I didn't have time to grieve because I had to get Cody ready for college. He was attending St. Cloud State University which was a three-and-a-half-hour drive away from home. I was excited for Cody, but sad for me. I was trying my best to prepare for his departure but my mind wouldn't wrap around it. Five weeks after Jim went home, Cody left for college. I was alone for the first time in eighteen years.

I dub the summer of 2010 as My Summer from Hell. Besides graduation, Cody's surgery and Jim's death, we also had some other things happen to us. The last weekend of June, my garage was broken into. They stole money from both my and Cody's cars and other belongings which included both of our iPods. When I was in Pittsburgh with Jim in July, my computer crashed and my washing machine broke. Then the first weekend of August, the hottest days of the summer, my air conditioner quit working and I had to replace it.

I truly believe God doesn't give us more than what we can handle, but that was a lot that summer. The phrase I kept repeating every time something would happen was, "Bring it on, bring it on. The more you bring on, the more I can handle." I always said it with a smile on my face too. I wasn't going to let the devil win. Thankfully, living in a small town and having a lot of family and friends around really helped. I have fantastic support. The kindness of people really showed through all of that; I am truly blessed.

One of my favorite quotes (from the book *P.S. I love You*) is: "Life is teaching you some painful lessons but it's from adversity that strength is born. You may have lost an inning, but I know you'll win the game."

There were two of Cody's friends going to the same college he was. Those two kids had single moms and now I was one again too. The three of us followed each other up to St. Cloud. On the way home, one of the other moms and I chatted almost the whole trip. She must have known I needed that. She was my guardian angel. We hung up about thirty minutes before arriving home. Once I entered our town I could feel the tears start welling up and once I turned down my street they started flowing. I could hardly see my house through my tears as I turned into my driveway and opened up the garage door. I remember thinking, *Now what am I going to do?*

Once inside, I bawled my eyes out. I didn't think the tears were ever going to quit. This was the first time I really allowed myself to cry. I probably cried for two to three hours, sitting by myself. I didn't have time for grief before, but now it was coming nonstop. Another best friend from childhood, Michele, lives across the street from me. She came over to console me and then said, as any good friend would, "Clean yourself up. We are going out for a drink."

I said, "I can't. I can't do it."

She said, "You're going to."

I looked at her with tears in my eyes rolling down my face. "What am I going to do now?"

She said, "You're going to pick yourself up, you're going to keep doing your business, and you're going to keep moving on. You're a strong-willed woman and you will conquer this."

I thought to myself, *I sure hope she's right.*

I hated being alone. I was still working my business and I felt so isolated since I worked from home. My clients were absolutely wonderful to me; they gave me the time off that I needed, were there to talk and gave me the encouragement to keep fighting. I found strength in people calling me just to talk and listen to me. It was also nice to listen to other people's problems for once. It seemed like I had so many, and I felt blessed that I could offer support to others in their time of need too. Even though there were a lot of people there once Jim was gone, it was the people who called me afterward and the people who called me after Cody was gone to school who were my greatest strengths because they were the ones who were there to pick me up when I was down. They were the ones who gave me comfort in my time of need.

Convenience versus obedience for me is the difference between divorce and staying married. Convenience is being married just for the convenience of having someone in your life but not fulfilling your marriage vows. Obedience is a God-fulfilled promise. Convenience is the devil's way of winning.

For convenience's sake, there were so many times I wanted to run: when I first started my business, when Jim was sick, when Cody acted up some in high school. There were so many times I was fed up with my business and wanted to shut it down, because of clients' work, not having enough income, having too many expenses, stress, etc. These were the times I just wanted to run and say, "Forget it, I don't want this anymore, this is not what I signed up for, this whole marriage thing for better for worse, in sickness and in health…" But in the long run, the obedience won out.

I fulfilled my wife role, I fulfilled my business role, I fulfilled my mother role, and as hard as it was and as much of a gut-wrenching roller coaster ride as it was, it was worth it and I consider it a true blessing. I would not be where I am at today without the trials and tribulations that life has put me through.

Running a business from home, you have flexibility and you have time to give to family, as well as the time to give to appointments or hospital stays or whatever is needed. You also have to remember your faith, no matter what that is.

Faith is remembering I am God's priceless treasure
when I feel utterly worthless.

Pamela Reeve.

There were so many times when I felt utterly worthless. I felt like a horrible business owner and I felt like a horrible nurse, even though in Jim's eyes I was his nurse. I felt like a horrible mother because I was trying to give Cody good, normal teenage years with stability and love.

I wanted a normal business, I wanted a normal husband; I just wanted everything normal, when in reality nothing in our life was normal. You make your own normal; you take what God has given you and you make that your normal.

The definition of *fortitude* is: "mental and emotional strength in facing difficulty, adversity, danger, or temptation courageously." That was me. I had fortitude and I used it to the best of my ability. I can't think of another thing that described me better during this time of my life.

I don't know if I was courageous or not. People thought I was crazy when I started my business but I'm so glad that I did because it's something out of the ordinary, or was at the time. When dealing with an illness face to face, fortitude is what keeps you moving forward. You have to find that emotional and mental strength to keep fighting and keep hanging on until the end. I look back at our situation now and see how I was trying my best to hang on while Jim was slowly slipping away.

Some days all I could do was drive out to the country and scream and cry. I would find a dirt road or back highway and just start crying my eyes out. I yelled at God and I yelled at the world. I was angry because I had finally found a wonderful man and he slipped away from us. Why was this happening? I didn't understand. If something better was coming, I surely couldn't see it at that time. Once I was home and calmed down I would ask for forgiveness from God and try and move on. Life was still happening and I had to be part of it. Getting the frustrations out also helped keep me moving forward.

The one thing I always counted on was my faith. I knew it was always working on my behalf and it is a priceless treasure from God. What we can't see or don't know are sometimes blessings in disguise.

Lean on, trust in, and be confident in the Lord with all your heart
and mind and do not rely on your own insight or understanding.
(Proverbs 3:5 AMP)

CHAPTER 10
Moving Forward

Be whole. How whole you are will determine the man or woman you attract in your life.

- Toyin Abiola

MOVING FORWARD can always be a difficult thing for some people. Me, in particular. I like change; however, at this particular instance in my life I really wasn't liking the change at all. Moving forward after Jim passed away and Cody went away to college was really difficult for me. I put a lot of pressure on myself, thinking about what I could've done differently to try to save Jim.

When you work from home like I do, you don't talk to a lot of people. I get up and I go to work and some days I would just sit there. I would sit there and stare at the computer and I couldn't focus, I couldn't concentrate. Thankfully, my clients understood that there were days that were harder than others.

I had some really good friends and family who would call me. I remember one particular friend in Texas, called me on a Monday. We sat and we talked for three hours. We laughed and cried. She was a widow as well. She just let me talk. She asked me questions when I couldn't talk anymore. Then she told me about her story. I remember thanking God that there were people like her in this world. I had other friends. I had one of my best friends, also named Michelle, call me on a different Monday. We just talked. She had no idea just before she called that I had been crying my eyes out, because I didn't know what to do or how to go about my next task or what I was going to do next.

Those are the types of things you just have to keep going. People say all the time, *"Take one day at a time."* Well, some days, taking one day at a time is too much. I made up this quote to fit my situation and it is my mantra now: *"Take one day at a time. If that's too much, take an hour at a time. If that's too much, just take one minute at a time."* Even if you have to do thirty seconds at a time, do that, but never give up.

Celebrate when you pass that second, minute, hour or day milestone. Tell yourself, okay I made it. I can keep going on to the next minute, and the next, and the next.

There were days, trust me, when even going a minute at a time was hard, but I did it. You just have to keep stepping and moving forward. If you're lonely, call people. Reach out to people. That's what I did. Even when I didn't think I could, it was funny how people actually reached out to me. They just knew. They just knew I needed somebody to talk to, and they were so good about it. I try to reciprocate that way with others now. If I know they are going through hard times, I reach out to them.

When I was going through my grieving process, I was really beating myself up, saying, *What could I have done?* I was on Facebook chatting with a gal from high school who was a couple of years older than me. She asked me how I was doing. I vented about how I wish I could have saved him, and how I wish I'd done more, etc. Sometimes when you least expect it, someone will put words into perspective for you and it will really hit home. She did that for me. She just said, "Jo, he gave you the gift of freedom. He knew he didn't want to suffer anymore, and he knew you didn't have to take care of him anymore. He is free of his pain and now you're free."

Wow. Point on. She was right, but I was mad after I reread it. I didn't want to know that I had freedom and that he had freedom. Yes, I was very happy he no longer had to suffer. I was very happy that he was in a better place, but I was also angry because I was left behind. I had to pick up the pieces. Now with Cody being away at college and being by myself, it was really hard. The more I thought about it, and the more it sunk into me and I thought, *She's right. He gave me the gift of freedom.* I no longer had to worry about him. I no longer had to worry about his medications. I no longer had to worry about hospitalization. I just no longer had to worry.

Even though I still worried about Cody, that intensity of worrying wasn't quite as bad because he was away at college. I couldn't see what he was doing every day, and every minute. I hated being an empty nester. I hated that Jim was gone, but I knew that was how God had done it. I'm a firm believer in God and that there are plans for all of us. I knew for some reason that was where I was supposed to be in my life. I couldn't explain why. I still don't know why but I slowly learned to accept it.

I'd read my Bible and pray every day. I became a lot more spiritual. I had always gone to church, but I became more spiritual. That summer really threw me for a loop. The grieving process is so hard to go through. There is anger and sadness, but then happiness because you remember all the good times. Then you're weeping. Then you want to scream out loud. Then it comes full circle again.

I did all that while working from home. When I went out in public you would never know I was grieving. I always put on a happy smile and tried to be pleasant. People knew I was sad but I don't like to dwell on my own life when I know others have it so much worse than I do.

When I was first by myself after Jim died and Cody went to college, I kind of just stayed secluded. I didn't want to run into anybody. I didn't want anybody to see me. Yet I knew I had to be out with the people, or I would go crazy sitting inside my house working. I only wanted to go where there would be laughter or one-on-one conversation. We had a coffee house in town and I found myself going there more and more with people. There was also a group that went out for happy hour on Tuesdays that I was invited to. I decided to join in. I knew it was only an hour but it was worth getting out of the house. I started coming out of my shell and was becoming more and more "me" again. It really was a healing process.

Another lifesaver for me at the time was my three dogs. They were always happy to see me and still gave me responsibility to care for and love something. They nourished me with their unconditional love. One of them has passed now, but I still have the other two. When we first got them, Jim thought I was crazy for having three dogs, but in the end that is what helped keep me sane.

In late September 2010, I decided it was time to do some home renovations. I was bored working all of the time and decided I needed something else to focus my mind on. We had a problem with our fence. Jim had put it up but it was kind of crooked. I decided I was going to do a new fence in my backyard. I spent my time interviewing different companies and finalizing plans. The fence got put up. Then I decided to paint inside my house and get some new furniture. I decided to use up some of my savings and make myself feel better.

The weird thing is I felt guilty at first. I really felt guilty because Jim and I would always talk about our finances and how we were going to do this, and how we were going to do that. For the longest time we talked about doing these projects. We just never got them done. It's weird that I would feel guilty, but I did. I felt like I had to get his permission or that he would be upset I was spending the money. I knew he was gone and wouldn't know about it, but that instinct just kicked in. I had to talk myself into doing these things. I wanted his acknowledgement that I was doing well in my choices and yet no one was there. The realization came that the choices now were all mine.

The more I resisted, the more I knew I needed to let go. Let go and let God. It took me about four months before I could start cleaning out his clothes. Some people told me to do it right away, while others said do it when you feel you are ready. I chose the latter. Most of the cleaning out was self-healing but when it came to disposing of his beloved leather jacket, I broke down. I smelled it and clung onto it as if he was still there. I couldn't let it go right away. My mother's friend works with a homeless mission that was looking for jackets that year. I decided to donate Jim's beloved jacket. I hoped someone could use it. A few months later, my mother informed me that the man who received it wears it every day and that he loves that jacket so much that he hides it until he wears it the following day. What a true blessing I felt for this man who could cherish that jacket as much as Jim did. Sometimes it's the small things in life that can really help someone else out in their time of need.

After Jim died, I went to six months of counseling and a grief support group. It was good to talk to others who were experiencing the same thing as I was. That also helped me see things from a whole new perspective. As we grieve, time keeps marching along. I got anxious about the future and wanted to know where my future would take me. I knew it was all in God's hands and according to his timing.

Something else I had wanted to do since my college years was obtain my Master's Degree. The fall after Jim died, I decided I was going to go for it. It gave me something else to devote my attention to and would get me out meeting other people. I decided to work on a Master of Business degree with an emphasis on entrepreneurship.

In January of 2011, I went back to school. I had to take a couple of undergrad classes because I didn't take them in my regular college courses. I ended up in those classes with a bunch of eighteen-, nineteen-, and twenty-year-olds. Their energy, their enthusiasm, their zest for life was exactly what I needed. They will never know how much they helped me get through those eight months of my life.

In September, once I was done with those classes, I started my regular program. I was one of the oldest in this group and they didn't have as much zeal for life as the younger ones had. We all had lives outside of college classes. Being with the younger college kids earlier on in the year really made me come alive. People started to notice. They said, "You're really starting to come back. You're being yourself again, and you're really coming back to life."

When I was married, I had a different last name. I took his name because he always wanted a wife with his last name. After he passed away, I decided to change my name back so my last name could match my son's. I took on a new identity with a new last name. It was okay, because I was the same person. This time I did it for me.

There are some days when you can be just fine, and other days when it just hits you like a rock. Most days, I was getting better and better, but there were some days it would just hit me and I would almost stand still. Just frozen on the spot. I could be in a grocery store and find something that Jim loved to eat, and I would just stand there and freeze. The tears would start rolling down my face. The grief process can be really, really tough, but it also can be a stepping stone to your next ventures in life. Every time there is a hurricane, there's also going to be triumph on the other side.

Going back to school after being out for twenty-five years was a huge step for me. People couldn't believe I was going back to school. I said, "It's something I always wanted to do and I just decided that I'm going to take time for me. I'm still going to run my virtual assistant business, but I'm going to take time for me and what I want to do. I've been taking care of everybody else all these years and it's time for me now."

In the spring of 2011, I was approached about running for our local City Council position. I was approached by a gentleman who I knew well and he had served on the council previously. I told him I didn't know a thing about City Council. He reassured me I would be good at it and it did spark my interest. So I decided to throw my name in the hat and run for City Council. After getting the necessary signatures for the ballot, I turned it in. The next week I found out I was the only one who took out a petition so I automatically won. I was excited and elated about this new chapter of my life. I won re-election in the spring of 2015 and continue to sit on the City Council as the Alderwoman for Ward Two of the City of Brandon, South Dakota.

Life was progressing along and I enjoyed sitting on the City Council. In 2012, I was approached by the same gentleman who got me to run for Council. He asked if I would be interested in running for our state House of Representatives. Again didn't know much about it, so after doing my homework on it, I decided to throw my name in for that election. It took a lot of time and energy but it was worth every minute. I met a lot of people on the campaign trail. It also took me out of my comfort zone. I placed large picture signs along the roads in my district. My name and picture were plastered all over my district. I was on public television and was entered into political debates. People recognized me from those signs. Running for State House of Representatives got me competing against some strong candidates who I had to fight to win. It was a tough battle. In the end I lost the election, but never gave up the fight. I continue to be active in my political party and have done other things for our community because of it. I can safely say I will never regret running for political office.

If you can step out of your comfort zone it really is an eye-opening experience. It's freeing. Be confident in who you are. If you're a risk-taker, then go out and take those risks. Just know who you are, be true to yourself. Giving me the gift of freedom was exactly what propelled my life forward in a positive way. I would have never guessed that would have happened after the summer of 2010.

I was scared to do all of the new things I was challenging myself with. But without risk there are no rewards. I was scared of the negativity that came from the political field. Yes, I received some, but it also brought forth positive people and things into my life. I stepped way out of my comfort zone to do them. While out in public, I had to be always on my toes and think like a winner. I enjoyed meeting new people, shaking their hands and hearing what they had to say. Although I lost the political race for State House of Representatives, I won at life.

Through every storm comes a rainbow and it has not been any less true for me. Don't let your emotions or negative self-talk get the best of you. If fear gets in your way, do what you need to do to overcome it. I also listened to my gut. If it said don't do something, I didn't. I was asked to buy businesses and I was asked to invest in real estate. Yes, I have done some of these things, but there were so many others that I have not. Be true to yourself and don't let your emotions get the best of you.

When you're having a bad day, honor that. Grief symptoms can be tough. If you're having a bad day at work, whatever it is that's happening in your life, honor that. Honor it, but don't dwell on it. When I was in a grocery store and I'd see a favorite food of Jim's, or I smelled his cologne somewhere, I would just stop. Cherish the time and move on. If you wake up and you're crabby, and you just don't think you can go on that day, then read the Bible, journal, exercise or do what you need to do to overcome it. I like to journal to get my feelings out. Then as time passes I go back and look how far I have come.

In my virtual assistant business, when I work with clients they have a team built around them. So along with working with the client I also work with other members of the team. Although there were many projects I could have completed for the client, they outsourced it to others while I worked on something different for them. I didn't like it and would say something to them. Most of the time they would agree with me but go ahead with their plans anyway. I had to learn to let go of control. When Jim was sick, I had to learn to let go of control. The doctors and God were in charge and all I could do was my best in order to take care of him. There are times you have to let go. There are times you have to let other people handle things that you cannot handle on your own. If you try to control too much, you lose clients, you lose money and you lose self-respect.

It's okay to let go of some of the reins. Once you do, you're going to find that you have a lot more freedom to work on your business instead of in your business. It really is a freeing feeling. Once you can let go of some of that control, it's freedom. Always remember, and never forget, be true to yourself. Always remember that gut is what's going to make you or break you. Always listen to your gut. Honor when you're having that bad day. Honor it, honor it, honor it. Never let it get the best of you. Also learn to let go of that control because someday, that control will take you over. You don't want that to happen. You want to be able to let go of that control, so you can let others help you.

CHAPTER 11
Achieving My MBA and Cody's BS

Desire is the key to motivation but it is determination and commitment to unrelenting pursuit of your goal, a commitment to excellence, that will enable you to attain the success you seek.

Mario Andretti

SINCE THE time I graduated from college, I had wanted to attain my master's degree. Desire was my motivation for my achieving my MBA. It didn't matter how long it had been, I just knew that I wanted to do it and the timing was perfect to start. I really had to believe that I deserved it. I do deserve it, and I did deserve it.

But first things first: I had to get over my fear of success. A lot of people will say, "Don't you mean fear of failure?" No, I've got that one pretty much down. I have failed several times in my life. Now it was time for me to get over my fear of success. It is an internal barrier that I set up for myself. To me, going through my master's degree classes was overcoming that fear. I wanted to quit so many times. I was going to quit a class because it was hard or I didn't want to do the homework. I wanted my new life back. But I didn't quit. I focused on me. I worked on me. I was determined to finish no matter what.

Even though there were so many times I wanted to be done I'm so glad now I didn't quit. It was a self-fulfilling prophecy that I could get my master's degree and I envisioned myself walking across the stage to receive it. I really kept that vision in place in my head and just knew that when that time came, it was going to be a phenomenal feeling. Sure enough, it was. March 6, 2014 was my last day of my classes and what a joy it was.

Did I believe I deserved this? How did I feel about it? To be honest I questioned it for a long time. Am I good enough for this? I really had to dig deep down inside of my gut and tell myself that I did deserve it. I'll be honest, I had friends who would say, "Yeah, I wouldn't blame you if you wanted to quit." You have to get over those negative things.

My mom was actually very instrumental in this. She wanted to see me graduate. She always said, "Before I die, I want to see you graduate with your master's." She's still alive and she saw me graduate. I wanted to prove to her that I could do it and I did. Not that I have to prove that to her because she loves me unconditionally. I proved to myself and many others that I could do it.

When March 6, 2014 came around, our professor was kind enough to let us out of class early. When I walked out that door it was the best feeling in the world. It was the most freeing feeling I'd had in a while. The stress, the homework, the driving to class every Wednesday night was now done. A bunch of us from the class went out for an adult beverage and it was probably the best I've ever had. It was just a self-fulfillment that I cannot even explain. To know I had worked so hard for that goal for that many years was just wonderful. I made myself pass my internal barrier. On May 18, 2014, I walked across the stage and received my degree. It was better than I had imagined.

After Cody's sophomore year of college, he moved back to South Dakota and finished school locally. He received his college degree a week before me; it was on May 10th, which happened to be Mother's Day weekend. For a mother, and having your son graduate from college with honors is a really great feeling. It was good to know that I helped push him along and hopefully was a really good role model for him. Actually, it was pretty fun that we were in college at the same time and he could see how I was fulfilling my dream. I was so proud of him and what a great sense of accomplishment he had as well. Being a mom and seeing your child succeed is an awesome feeling.

After college was over, I decided it was time to use my master's degree. Along with doing my virtual assistant work, I thought I needed to get out of the house more. I needed to have a little retail shop or something that I could do part-time. As a virtual assistant, you can take your work with you wherever you go. As long as you have a laptop or iPad you're pretty much set. I knew the U-Haul business was getting sold and so I decided to open up a U-Haul business in my town. In the retail space that I rented, I had about 500 square feet that was not being utilized. I did some checking into what would work in my town. I decided to do a booth rental store and call it Jojo's Closet. My new businesses were born.

Opening up the stores was a big accomplishment because I always thought I'd be sitting at home, working at my business and doing my thing on my computer. I'm such a people person that I knew deep down I had to be out with people. I knew that one of my desires and my goals in life was to be with people. I thought about maybe a coffee shop since I love coffee, but I didn't want the hours associated with that.

Running a U-Haul business is something I thought I would never do. I don't like working on trucks or even know much about them. But with anything, we learn as we go. Yes, I get up in those trucks and I clean them and I sweep them out. I do everything that you're supposed to do with a U-Haul. I take care of the customers. I do all the paperwork. Really, it is a fun gig. Plus, my biggest thing is I'm out with people and I get that personal connection. That brings me strength. That brings me dignity. That brings me pleasure. Being a virtual assistant had always brought me pleasure. I love my virtual assistant work but this brings me that personal interaction that I need on a daily basis.

In October 2014, Cody decided to move to Colorado. I was all in favor of it because as a mother you want to see your kids excel. You want to see your kids move on to the next level in their life and I knew living here with me, in my house, was not providing him what he needed to grow and to learn about what it's like out there in the real world. When he asked me if I thought it would be okay to move to Colorado, I said go. Do it. Expand your wings. Go and fly and have a great time. You're young, you're free, you don't have any kids or a marriage. I really encouraged him to go out there and expand his wings. That's exactly what he did. He is doing fantastically and as a mother, I couldn't be more proud of him.

Once he moved I found myself alone again. One of my biggest fears was being alone again. I am somebody who likes to have a lot of people around, who likes that social interaction all the time. I loved having him with me but, again, he was old enough, and he had to be out on his own. Overcoming my fear of being alone has been a blessing. With every goodbye, we learn and we grow. I grew a lot as a person, mother and business owner after he left. I now had to rely on myself again and I found out who my true friends were. I had so many people come to me and ask if they could help, and this time I let them. I found time to meditate, read my Bible daily and journal more than I had been. I found me and it is great.

Is it easy every time? No. Are there lots of days I wish I wasn't doing it? You bet. As a business owner, I think all of us think that way. Even when you're working for somebody else you will think that way too. There are days I sit there and think, *What the heck am I doing? Why am I doing this?*

Then I think, *That's right, I want the freedom to have and set my own hours and do my own thing.* That is exactly what I've worked for and that's exactly why I got my master's degree. It's just the best feeling in the world knowing that I have people coming to my store because they want to see me and they want to see what I have in my store. They come back for the customer service. They've told me that repeatedly.

I see people out in public and they will say, "Hey, you own Jojo's Closet," or, "You run U-Haul."

I smile and say, "I sure do."

One of my biggest assets is that I like to make a difference for others. Running the store is also helping vendors get their products and goods out there. To me that's healing. In a way, that's giving back to others. I'm making a profit off it because I'm not going to go without making money, but it fulfills my prophecy of being able to help others fulfill their dreams. Sometimes we just have to trust and fly without a net. That's scary. As scary as that can be, that's what happens. When I was left alone and I encouraged Cody to go, I just had to learn how to do it on my own.

Again, it goes back to my favorite quote that I reworded to fit my situation:

*You wake up, show up, throw up if you must,
but don't you dare ever give up.*

– Jo Hausman.

I had to keep repeating that in my mind over and over and over again. The more I knew that I could do it on my own, the stronger I got. The more self-fulfilled I got.

Opening up a retail store really showed me that I could do it on my own. I'm not in the same mindset I was in when I was in my twenties and wanted to prove to the world who I was. Now I'm proving who I am to me. I know if I focus on myself and become a better person for me and God, that's going to bring the right people into my life. Be it a man, be it friends, be it customers or vendors, as long as I'm happy with myself and I know that I've worked on myself and that I have done what's best for me, then those right people will come around.

So far it's working fantastically. Life is good. I also got back into working out again. I started kickboxing again. Kickboxing is something I've done for years on and off. What a mindset you can get from just exercising your body that will also exercise your mind. It will put your mind at ease. It will calm anxieties. It will bring you back into focus. It will help calm fears.

I go to kickboxing three days a week and I will say I'm probably the happiest now that I've ever been. My friends and family tell me I look great and they've never seen me smile so much. I smile so much on the outside because I feel so happy and content on the inside. It's a peace that I've never felt before in my life. It's almost like a self-fulfillment peace that brings out, I believe, the best in me. I know that I can fulfill these goals and dreams like I want to fulfill them. When people ask me what my secret is, I just tell them peace. Peace which passes all understanding. It is just a phenomenal place to be. For years I ran; not away from things, but since I was focusing so much on husband, son, parent, mom, and then family and friends, I just never really got to work on me.

I've been taking the time to do that and it really has been a great accomplishment, bringing a great, enduring love for myself that I never thought I would have. It has opened up my eyes to a lot of new and fun things in my life that I never thought I'd get to do again. I've gotten to a place of peace and understanding in my life that cannot be taken away.

Some achievements include getting the courage to go out and make some real estate investments. When Jim and I were newly married, we wanted to start investing in real estate. Through our time together we bought one rental house. When he was sick, we sold it. Now I was getting the urge to buy again. I opted for a rental place and then found another and another. The more you do, the more confident you become. I think that also comes from the peace that lies within me. I don't rush to buy real estate now. I take my time, look around and put a lot of thought into it before I buy. I'm also able to share my experiences with other people.

The year of 2014 was a year of release. Once I learned to release what was holding me down, a whole new world appeared. I found me again - a new and improved me.

I could do the real estate, a political career or business ventures by myself, but I don't. I ask for assistance. I seek others to help me come to terms with what I am dealing with. I like it when people are honest and open with me. I now know that the right people will come into my life. Some have, and always will, stay and a lot have come and gone. But every friendship, new and old, is a gift I have been given and I cherish it. Because of that gift I am truly blessed. I thank my God every day for all the blessings he has given me. One of my prayers I pray daily is to have him remove the negativity from my life and have only fun, positive things and people enter. It is also a mindset. If I truly believe that will happen, It does.

Another prayer I say every morning and evening is thanking God for healing my heart, my mind, my body and my soul. I listen to my God, I listen to my body and I listen to my universe. Because of the peace that now surrounds me in my life, joy and wonderful things continue to happen. I'm looking forward now to the next chapter of my life.

My internal qualities kept me going, and they were tenacity and determination. We all have them; it is just a question of using them. When you are running your own business there will be many days when you will probably want to quit, or there will be many times when you may have a million things going on and you don't know which way to go.

Sometimes, if you're like me, you like the idea of starting a business but once the business gets going, you get really bored with it. The thing is, that's when the tenacity and the determination really come into play. Even when you're starting the business, it doesn't matter which area you are in, you have to keep going with that tenacity and determination. Don't ever let other people's thoughts or negative actions get in your way. If there are days when you're bored sitting at the office or sitting at your business, do things to help market your business. Do things that are going to help promote it.

I can't stress that enough because there are days when you just want to sit there and not do a darned thing. You just hope people walk in the door. It might happen, but it's not going to happen if you don't tell people that you're there. You really have to get out there. You really have to make yourself be determined and get out there and tell everybody you know what you do for a business.

Probably more than anything, you need to believe in yourself. People are going to come into your store or they're going to come into your business, and maybe they're not going to really need what you have to offer, but they're going to buy because they believe in you. You need to believe in yourself. Before they can believe in you, you need to believe in yourself. Do what you need to do to make you feel good doing that business. Don't be a liar, don't be a cheater, don't do any of those of things. Do something honest and favorable. Once you have that belief in yourself, there's nothing that can stop you.

Also learn to take risks. A lot of people can have the belief and they can have the tenacity and determination, but they're scared to take that risk. If all of us were scared to take risks, we wouldn't be where we are today. That means financially, or physically, or whatever. It was scary to me when I had to start paying rent on a leased space. That was a risk for me. For years while working my virtual assistant business, I pondered if I should be in an office space instead of my home office. I always answered no and kept working from home. That's the kind of thing you need to do to take risks. Some of them are more calculated than others, but just learn to take those risks and do what you need to do to step one foot forward.

To wrap it all up, just know that tenacity and determination are key factors when you need to really get in the game and get your business off the ground and going. Even if it becomes stagnant, go after those customers, go after that market share, but go after whatever you need to do in your business. Believe,in yourself and believe that you can get it done. If you don't believe in yourself, nobody else is going to believe in you. You really need to believe in yourself. Also, take those risks. Take those risks that are going to put you one step forward and put you on the road to eternal success.

My Conclusion

SOMETHING MY mother has always said to me is, "You must heal your past before you can move to your future." When I was younger, I just let that phrase go in one ear and out the other. As I grow older, and more life experiences have happened to me, I'm truly starting to believe it. Sometimes, we may feel like we want to move forward and are healed, but something is holding us back. A lot of times, it could be past memories or past things that have happened in our lives. We only allow them to control us in the present. The memories are only in our minds and that is what controls us.

To gain control over those past memories, don't define yourself by what happened. I've had to learn this myself. Redefine how you're going to manage your thoughts and actions. I thought, *Okay, how am going to gain control over my past, so I can move to my future?* Yes, I try new things. Yes, I'm blazing new trails. How do I get those memories from my past out? One way for me is to talk about my past relationship with my husband and how he loved Cody and me unconditionally.

When I meet someone who has lost a spouse, or perhaps they're going through a hard time, I tell them our story. I recently had supper with a gal who lost her husband a few months ago. I tell my story. I'm healing my past along with helping others. It's a great joy for my soul that I can give of myself in this way. My hope is that they can find hope and move on with their future.

No one has made me feel as loved as Jim did, before or since. I never worried about him leaving. I never imagined us ending our marriage for any reason other than death. He was the one person I fully trusted with all my heart. Living with that, knowing I did everything possible, gives me comfort. The way Jim loved us was a gift from God. God heals us in his time, not ours.

I've been told by several experts that healing our past also includes forgiving ourselves. It took me several months to forgive myself, because I always thought I could have done more for Jim. It wasn't until I did a lot of self-study, and self-healing, that I realized the gift of freedom is forgiveness.

I now live in freedom. I know that I can move forward each day and keep going forward because the end result would have been the same for Jim. I know that he's at peace now with our Lord, and that knowledge keeps me at peace. When the naysayers come forward and blame the VA or blame the doctors or whoever, I will reaffirm that there was nothing more that could have been done. I'm at peace knowing that I have healed my past.

People will run from problems. One of the hardest things to do is have staying power. I never liked to stay. When problems came up, I was the first one out of there. Strength grew from staying power. You have to be patient during the process because growth takes time. It has been several years since Jim has passed, and I'm still growing. I'm still learning. New experiences, new people come into my life every day. I love it. Most of them are positive, fun-loving people because that's what I'm attracting. That's what I put out to the Universe, and that's what comes back to me. That's what I want. I don't want negativity. I don't want drama in my life. I want peace, love, happiness and perseverance. Staying power isn't easy. Growth and healing take time. Every day is a learning experience.

As Mark Batterson writes in his book *All In*:

We Want Joy without Sacrifice

We want Character Without Suffering

We Want Success without Failure

We want Gain without Pain

We want a Testimony without Test

We want it all without going all out for it

Wouldn't it be nice to have it all without suffering? But what would we have? Nothing. Nothing to strive for. Nothing to achieve. Our lives would end up boring and mundane.

Look at each day as a treasured gift. When I wake up in the morning, I say, "Thank you, God, for today." I even state today's date, "Today is (today's date)," and, "Thank you, God, for (today's date). What a beautiful, sunshiny day." It could be snowing outside. "Hey, thanks for the beautiful snow today." My life begins every day that I wake up in the morning. I know when I get up, I'm on fire, and I am going to blaze through that day because I'm creating my future today and blazing new trails. Like I said, I look at each day as a treasured gift. I blaze new trails because I will write down what makes me excited, what makes me get up every day, what makes me feel alive every day.

You have to learn daily what is going to wake you up in the morning. Sometimes when you're in the thick of problems in your life, you might have trouble thinking of what excites you. There's nothing wrong with living and dreaming bold, bodacious dreams. Write them down. Eventually, they may come true. If not, what's the harm in writing them down? What's the harm in dreaming them? Because if you don't dream them, they're never going to come true anyway. You might as well dream them so they can come true.

I have a daily to-do list, and a daily dream list. I write down each day: my dream, my goal, where I want to go in this life. I know this is not where I'm going to be the rest of my life. I know greater and more wonderful things are coming and that I am just moving one step forward each day. I hold my head up high. I smile at everybody I meet. That's how I relate to this life because that's how I want people to remember me. That is also how I live my life. I know that bigger, and better, and bolder things are coming my way. When I blaze new trails I'm thinking, *Either you come along with me for the ride, or you move out of the way, because if you're not coming with me for the ride, I don't need your negativity. I don't need your self-doubt, or your doubt, because if you put doubt on me, sometimes that comes back as self-doubt. I don't need that in my life.*

Every morning and night I say my prayers. I read my daily gratitude journal and my daily devotion, and then I start writing. I write down what my big, bold, bodacious dream is for the day. Where do I want to go with my life? What do I want to do? What kind of people do I want to meet? If I could have the perfect life, what would it look like? If I hate my job, or my business, why should I remain in it? Why would I live like that? I wake up. I go to a business that I love doing. I love talking to new people. I love creating new ideas for people. I love helping people get to the next step in their life, and so they can live the big, bodacious dreams that they never thought possible. People helped me in the past, and now I'm paying it forward.

I pray for people. I pray for businesses. I only want blessings for people. That brings me peace because I don't wish evil on anyone. I only wish blessings, and peace, and gratitude. That helps me become a better person.

So, let everything you say be good and helpful so that your words will be an encouragement to those who hear them." (Ephesians 4:29)

If you do your own soul searching, research and investigation into what you want in your life, and then you go after it, you will not believe how wide open the doors will be; the more you will come alive and how things will fall into place for you.

People tell me a lot, "You're so strong. You're the most positive one." That's how I choose to live. I would rather be known as a trailblazer who likes to take life on with passion, purpose and fulfillment. That is what makes me alive and grateful for every day I am blessed to be on this earth.

Wake up every day with gratitude and find something in your life to look forward to. Maybe it is hanging with your kids or your spouse. Maybe gardening or lawn care. Maybe it's snow removal or doing crafts. Maybe you like to drive people to their different appointments. Do you realize each of those things can be turned into a small business? Be creative. Get out of your comfort zone and do something daring that will bring you closer to your dreams. Reinvent yourself. You never know how far you can go until you try something new.

I am proud of myself and the woman I have become today. It has not been easy. It takes a lot of guts to do what I have done and even though it comes naturally to me, it is still a big accomplishment. I don't jump into things. I look, plan, create and implement. It takes time. Losing both my dad and Jim at young ages really got me thinking about life. Losing Jim really propelled me. I can't tell you that I would have gone back and received my MBA, done more real estate, run for office or opened up new businesses while he was still alive. Losing him propelled me to want more in life and that life was too short to let opportunities pass me by. The two most influential men in my life gave me such a strong foundation and such a strong love that I know how proud they would be of both Cody and me. I know they are smiling down from heaven.

We never know how much longer we have on this earth. Even though some days seem endless, there are gifts given to us. Go forth and conquer each day as it comes because when death comes there are no second chances. It's final. Tell the people around you how much you love them. Find peace within yourself. Be grateful for what you have. Go for it and persevere. Never forget you're more powerful than you give yourself credit for.

About the Author

Jo Hausman

Jo Hausman holds a MBA in Business with Entrepreneurship from the University of Sioux Falls. She is a self-starter with tenacity and proven leadership skills. Her selfless acts of kindness for family, community and church are telltale signs of her true character. She owns several small businesses and is a real estate investor and city council alderwoman. She enjoys spending time with family and friends and is the proud mother of her son Cody and her 2 fur babies Dakota and Ellie.

She loves to help others in achieving their dreams and goals. She has trained dozens of people to become virtual assistants. As part of her giving back nature she has donated her time and talent to various organizations. She thrives to see people succeed and grow into their own being. Coaching them helps her see them succeed.

Cody Hausman

Cody Hausman holds a Bachelor of Science from South Dakota State University. He is a marketing coordinator for an industrial supplies company. He enjoys volunteering during election time, playing pickup basketball games and checking out new unique shops.

Made in the USA
San Bernardino, CA
28 February 2016